Date with an Artist

CONTENTS

We normally associate the commissioning of art with portrait painting or celebrating some major public event, or possibly making a new work especially for a temporary exhibition or another public place. But it was not always so: in the past it was common practice for patrons, whether the aristocracy, the Church, or newly wealthy burgers, to commission artists to make original work for a specific place - the chapel or the home - to a very specific brief.

While art today is no longer the preserve of the rich and powerful, it is still viewed by many as being somehow remote and irrelevant. This is a pity, as the best art encourages us to look anew at the way we live and addresses the big moral and spiritual questions. It is also a fact that artists, including those whose work is regarded as the most challenging and difficult to understand, draw on all kinds of familiar material and experiences - found objects and chance encounters, public affairs and private obsessions.

To try and re-establish the link between art and how we live now. Date with an Artist paired twelve of the country's most exciting artists with partners who might in some way inspire a new piece of work for the home. Those 'partners', chosen after discussion with the artists about the areas of interest they wanted to explore, were as varied as the kind of work that was produced, and include a bee-keeper, a prisoner, a musician, a house full of junior doctors and a vision scientist.

The whole project, initiated by BBC Arts, was only made possible through an unique collaboration between several organisations who share the common goal of bringing contemporary art to a wider audience. The BBC2 television series, first transmitted in December 1997, documents the twelve dates from initial meeting, through the devising and making of the work, to its final unveiling in the home of the patron. The series was co-produced with the Arts Council of England, who have an impressive track record of pioneering new ways of bringing the contemporary arts to the small screen.

But while television can be a very effective means of showing art in its context, and indeed of exploring work in photographic detail, it can never be a complete substitute for seeing it at first hand. The exhibition of the art works made for the BBC programmes can be seen at Northern Gallery for Contemporary Art in Sunderland and it offers the visitor an opportunity to judge the finished art works off screen at their leisure. Accompanying the series and exhibition this co-published booklet between BBC Arts, BBC Education Production and NGCA, acts as a comprehensive guide to the project as well as containing a provocative essay on the historical place of art in the home.

We are extremely grateful to all the participating artists for committing themselves to the project with such energy and enthusiasm, and to their dates for their various and varied contributions to the process, as well as their generosity in allowing us into their homes. With regard to how far - and how successfully - the artists have responded to their dates and the environment they inhabit, that is for the reader and viewer to judge.

Keith Alexander, Series Editor, Date with an Artist and Louise Wirz, Principal Curator, Northern Gallery for Contemporary Art, Sunderland,
December 1997

NTRODUCING the Artists & their Dates

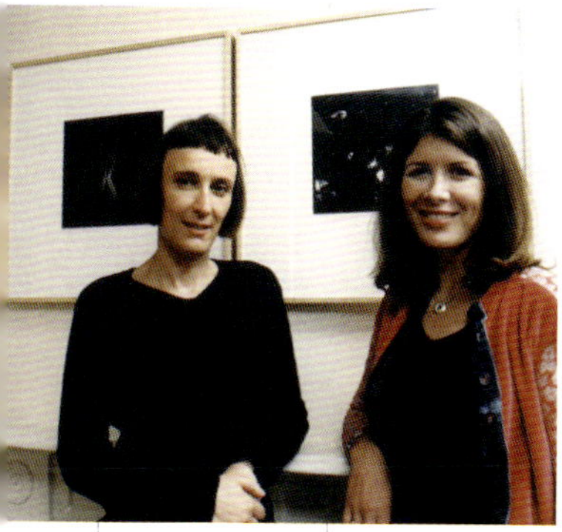

CORNELIA PARKER, who makes works with objects that have specific connections to people, places and things, meets Rebecca Stephens, the first British woman to climb Everest. Why is Cornelia interested in Rebecca's down jacket, and what will she find of interest on their own shared adventure – a trip up into the dome of St Paul's Cathedral?

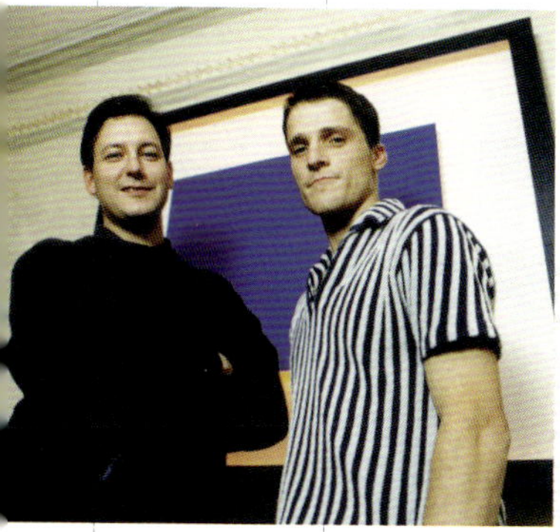

ANDREW GIFFORD, whose light installations and paintings of industrial landscapes are inspired by the special quality of the skies around his home town of Middlesbrough, meets Dave Allan, PR Manager for Middlesbrough Football Club. What will Dave want Andrew to paint? What will Andrew want to paint? And how will Dave react when he sees a light installation in his bedroom, instead of just the painting he was expecting?

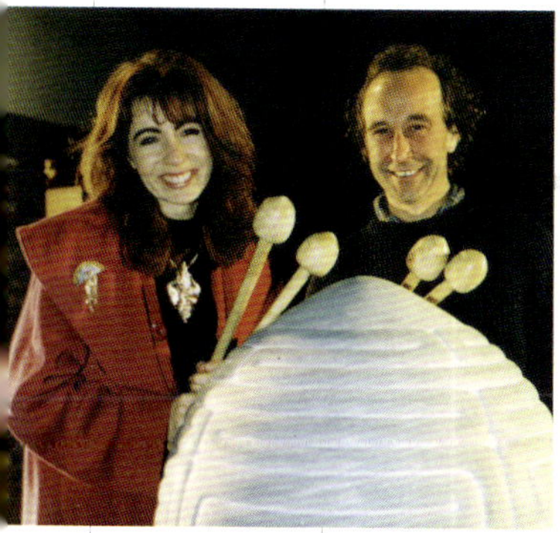

PETER RANDALL-PAGE, who is probably Britain's best-known stone-carving sculptor, meets Evelyn Glennie, the world-famous percussionist. Because Evelyn plays so many different instruments, she has a strong awareness of the relationship between the shape of an object and its sound – a relationship which is heightened by her own profound deafness. Can Peter take up the challenge to carve a sculpture that will resonate in such a way that Evelyn will be able to play it?

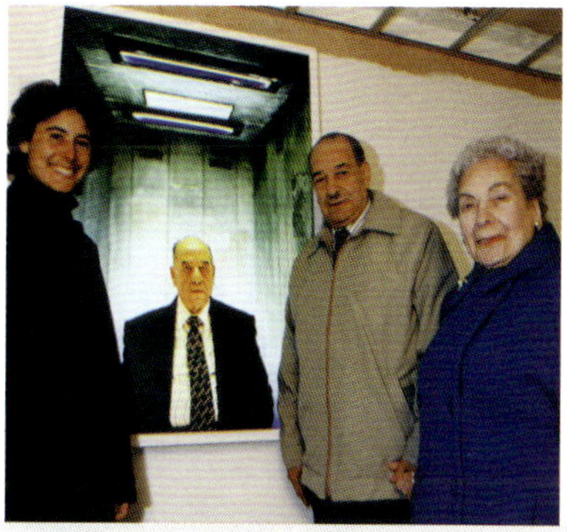

CATHERINE YASS, who displays her specially manipulated, colour heightened photographs in light-boxes, meets Mr Archer and Mrs French, two elderly Eastenders who are on the point of moving into a tower block that has been completely refurbished as a haven for the over-50s. How will the relationship between Mr Archer and Mrs French and their homes inspire Catherine? And will the couple like the photograph that Catherine takes?

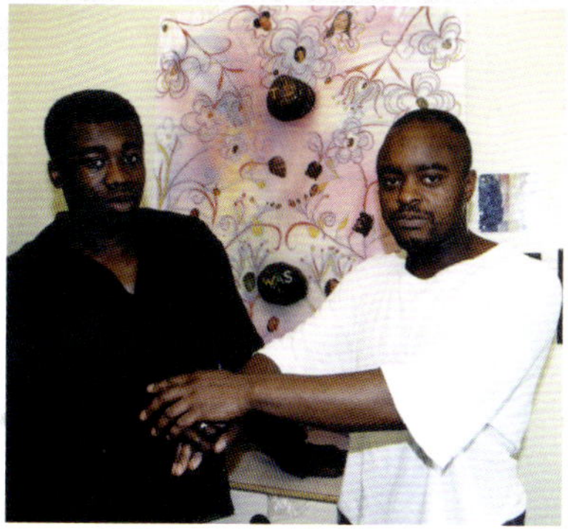

CHRIS OFILI, who makes colourful paintings embellished with varnished elephant dung, meets Anthony Ismond, a prisoner in Wormwood Scrubs, who shares Chris's passion for rap and hip-hop music. What will Anthony think of the painting Chris makes for him, which has his nickname, Tiswas, spelt out in pins in the dung? And how will Chris react to the experience of being inside a prison for the first time?

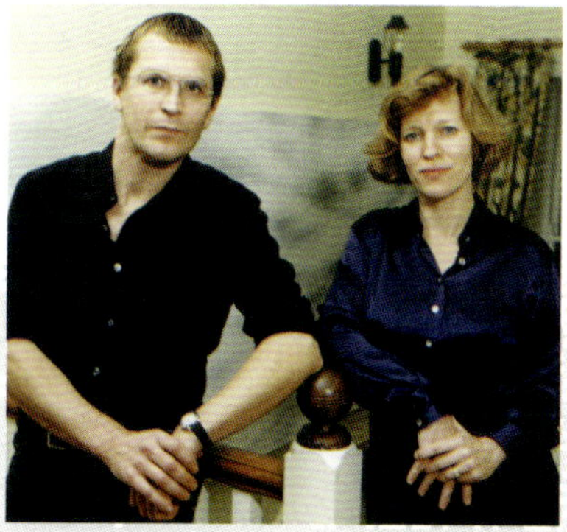

BRAD LOCHORE, who makes elegant and mysterious paintings of shadows, meets Anya Hurlbert, a vision scientist specialising in shadow perception and the way the eye distinguishes shapes. Who will know more about shadows – the artist or the scientist – and what will they learn from each other?

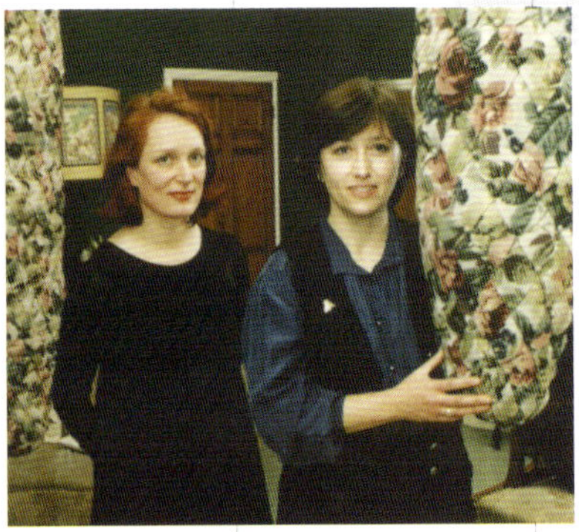

NINA SAUNDERS, who makes her sculptures by customising old bits of furniture in a very original and distinctive way, meets Sally Leslie, a beekeeper in Dorset. Can an old chair that Nina has found really be transformed into something that Sally will recognise as bee-like? What stage will it be in the lives of bees that appeals to Nina's imagination? And what will Sally think of the new art work in her sitting-room?

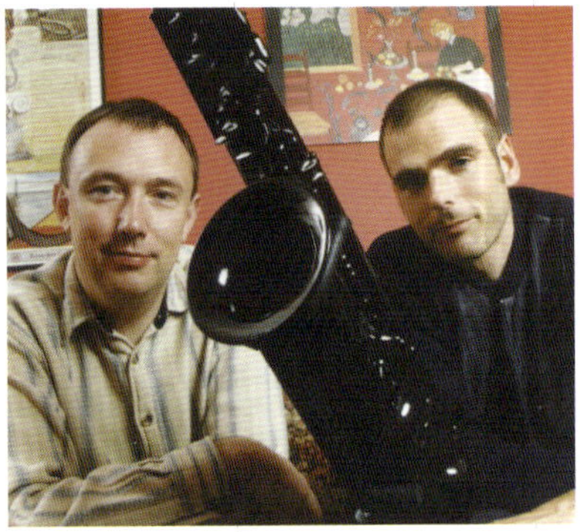

HADRIAN PIGOTT, who specialises in making dysfunctional objects, be it a camera that cannot photograph, or an unplumbed basin in which one cannot wash, meets John Butcher, an avant-garde saxophonist whose music Hadrian finds inspirational. John pushes the saxophone to its limit, attempting to play the unplayable by forcing his instrument to make noises it was not designed to make. How will Hadrian respond to this music, and what will John think of his new unplayable sculpture?

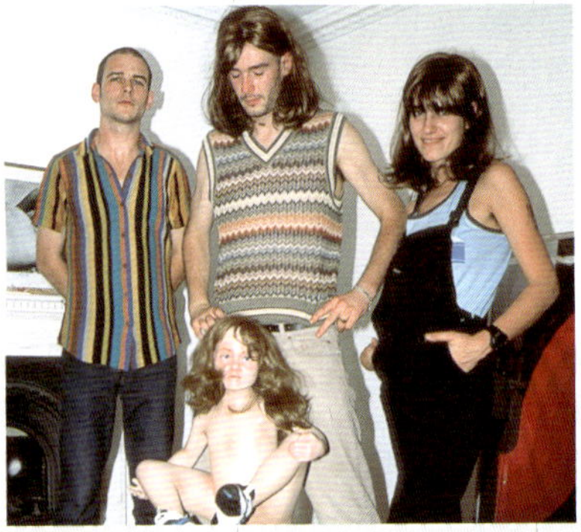

JAKE & DINOS CHAPMAN, internationally renowned for their sculptures of mutilated bodies and genitally abnormal child mannequins, meet Justine Frischmann from Elastica, one of Britpop's biggest stars. Where in her house will Justine choose to have her sculpture? And what will the Chapmans do if she doesn't want the sculpture they've planned for her?

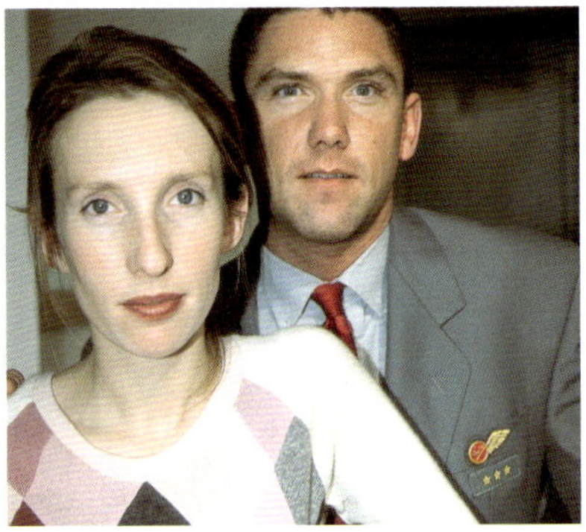

SAM TAYLOR-WOOD, who mak
photographs and films th
unsettle the viewer by playi
with identity and explori
unspoken tensions in hum
relationships, meets Alasta
Morrison, a chief steward for
major airline. Sam wants to u
Alastair's large loft-sty
apartment as a setting for one i
series of 360-degree photograp
of rooms that she is curren
making. Will Sam be able
incorporate Alastair successfu
into her photograph?

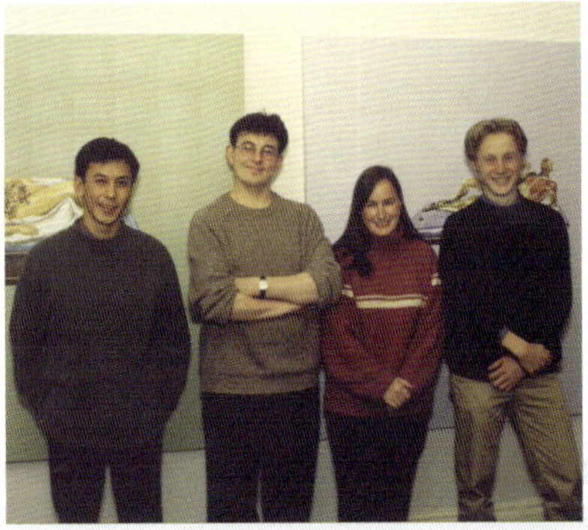

JULIE ROBERTS, painter
anatomical figures, psychologic
stories and medical instrumen
meets Ien Soun Ly, Bar
McKillop and Colin Begg, th
young doctors sharing a flat
Glasgow. Will they recognise t
body parts Julie paints? And w
they think that the mo
unappealing realities of their jo
in hospitals provide suitab
subject-matter for art on th
walls at home?

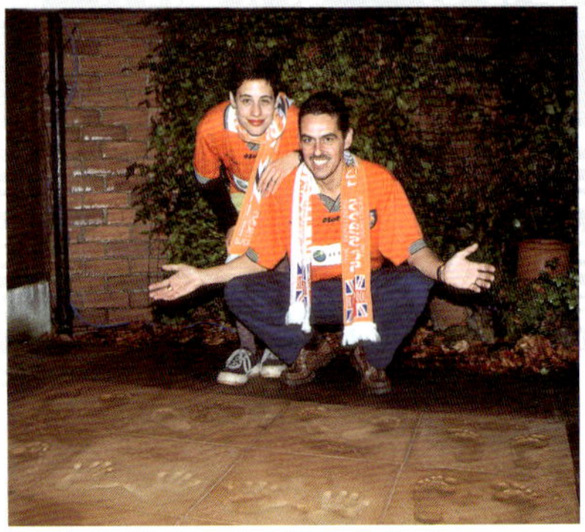

JESSICA VOORSANGER, who
work deals with celebrity and
relationship between famo
people and their fans, meets G
Cook, a devoted fan of Blackp
Football Club, who has be
watching the team since he w
four. Will Jessica persuade
football team to make prints
their feet in cold, sett
concrete? And will Gary like
new patio?

PAUL GLINKOWSKI:

BRINGING IT ALL BACK HOME

INTRODUCTION

Nowadays, when people think of art, particularly contemporary art, they may imagine spotless white galleries where security guards ensure that curious spectators keep their distance from the precious objects meticulously disposed around the floors and walls. Date With An Artist gave twelve contemporary British artists the chance to show that this is not the whole picture.

The story of Western art has tended to emphasise the gradual separation of art from the mainstream of life. According to the most pessimistic account, art, which began in a communal cave around 30,000 years ago, has ended up in a sterile white cube, and it has failed to take the public with it. Although it may sometimes appear this way to those who feel excluded from art, there have been many attempts throughout the history of art, particularly in recent decades, to bring art back closer to home. There are three ways in which this has happened: through subject-matter – what art is about; through materials – what art is made from; and through location – where art is seen and experienced.

In terms of subject-matter, scenes and aspects of everyday life, though not always highly valued by the art establishment, have inspired artists from all periods. This continues to be the case today. In terms of the raw materials from which art is made, artists have increasingly found that they can express their thoughts and feelings more vividly and effectively by using the stuff of everyday life. The idea that art should be made from specialist, often quite precious, materials, such as oil paint and marble, has been replaced now by a belief that anything can, potentially, be made into art, even a humble pile of bricks. In terms of location, although people immediately think of the art gallery or museum as the place where art belongs, many artists today are finding opportunities to show and make work beyond the confines of the gallery. Some hold exhibitions in disused shops or warehouses, some work directly with people in public places like schools or hospitals, others prefer to work outside in the environment, often making work from natural materials found on site. If we look closely around the towns, cities and countryside that we inhabit, we may be surprised to find that art today is often nearer to home than we might think.

FROM CAVES TO CUBES: in which art leaves home and enters the cathedral

The earliest paintings date back to the Ice Age when our ancestors took shelter in caves, like the famous caves of Lascaux in France or the caves of Altamira in Spain. We can only guess at the meaning of these first, often very vivid, images, of animals such as bison and deer. Perhaps primitive hunters believed they could gain power over their prey by capturing its likeness? It seems clear that, whatever their inspiration, these cave paintings had a very basic connection to the lives of those who made them.

During the time of the great pagan civilisations in Europe – the civilisations of the ancient Greeks and the Romans – we know that art still had a role in everyday life. Although little art work, particularly painting, survives from the Greeks, contemporary writings speak of masters who specialised in everyday subjects. We know about painting in Roman times from the decorative wall-paintings and mosaics which have been unearthed at Pompeii and other excavated sites. Pompeii, a well-to-do country town, was buried beneath the ashes of Vesuvius in AD 79. Almost every house and villa in Pompeii had paintings on its walls and columns; everything from still lifes to landscapes. Household items too, such as crockery, were decorated with intricate scenes.

Although art came increasingly to be identified with higher things – recording the portraits and deeds of secular princes and heroes as well as celebrating the lives of the holy – artists throughout the centuries have maintained an interest in the rituals and objects of domestic life. This was particularly so in 17th-century Holland, where still life and genre painting flourished. Perhaps the greatest exponent of genre painting, the depiction of scenes from everyday life, was Johannes Vermeer van Delft. Most of Vermeer's paintings are of individuals, such as *The Kitchen Maid*, going about their business in the rooms of typical middle-class Dutch houses. The meticulous attention given to each of the objects in his paintings – from a roll of bread, to an earthenware jug, to a basket hanging from the wall – make them like still lifes with people in them. Despite the humble subject-matter, their quiet beauty places them amongst the most popular and affecting of Old Master paintings.

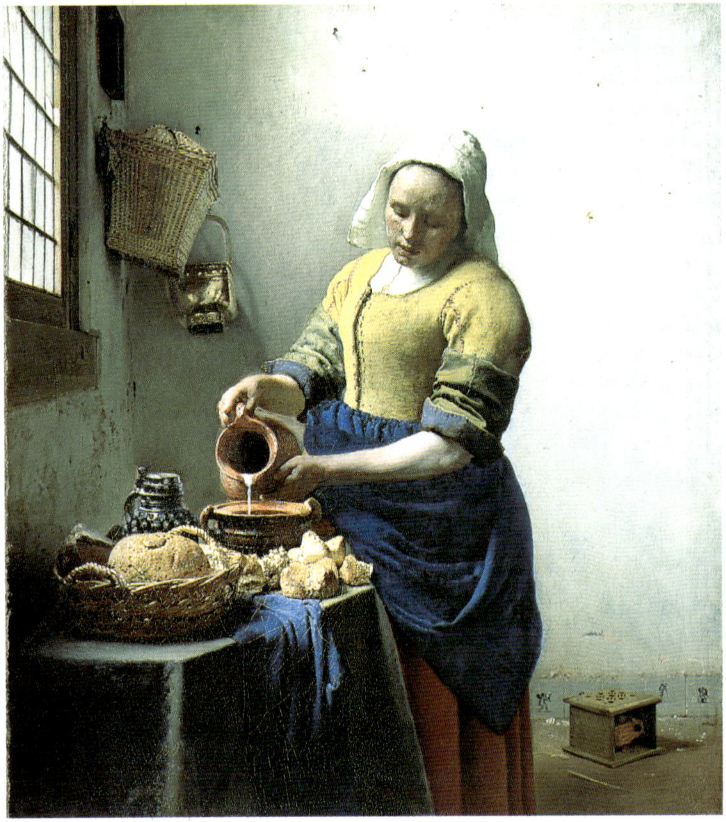

JOHANNES VERMEER,
THE KITCHEN MAID, C.1660
RIJKSMUSEUM, AMSTERDAM

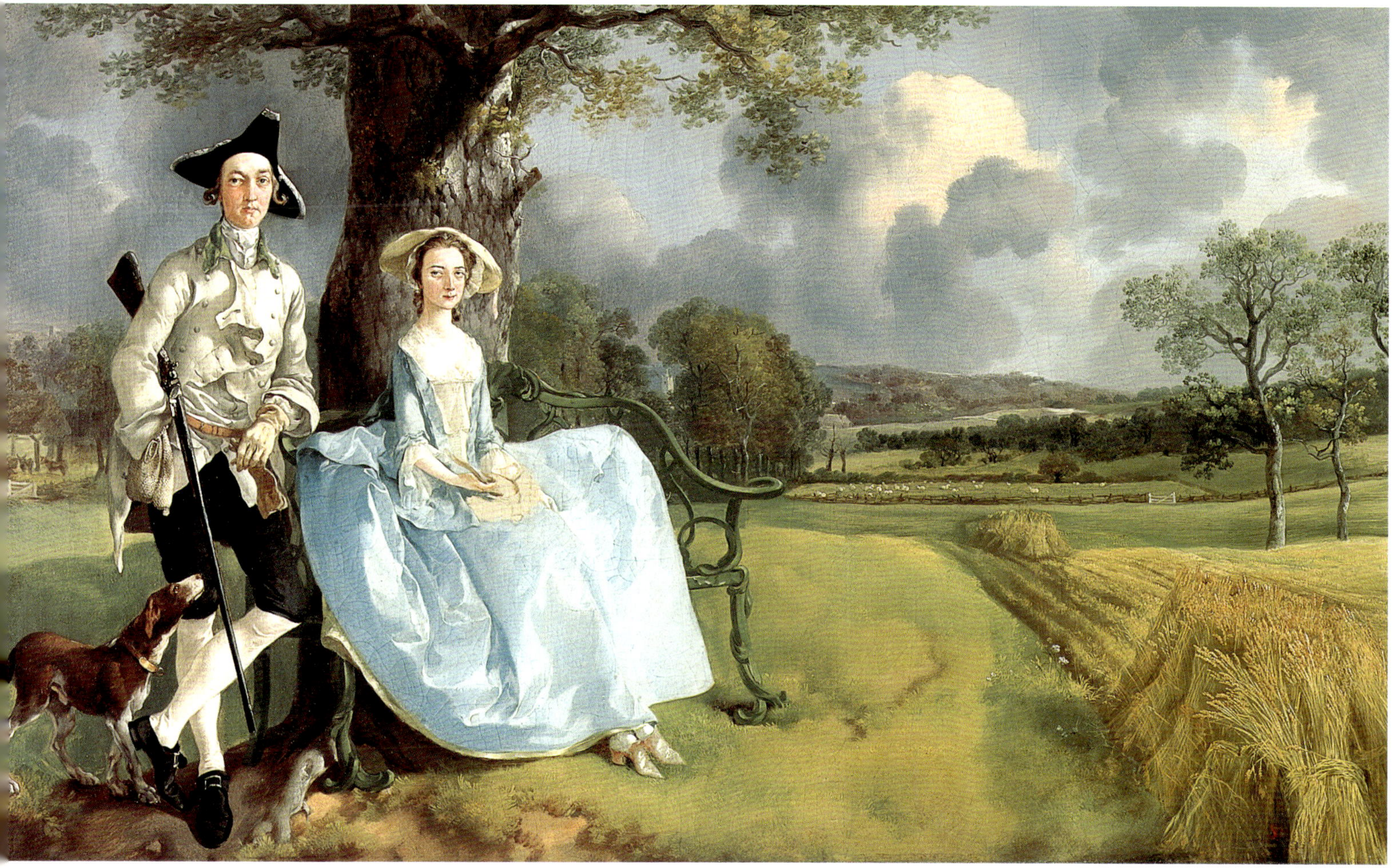

'he houses most usually depicted in Old Master paintings belonged to the rich and powerful. Paintings commissioned by the aristocracy, of their homes ınd possessions, were meant to celebrate their splendour and superiority and to refute any idea of kinship with 'the common man'. This point was well made by the critic John Berger in his 1972 television series *Ways of Seeing*, in which he attempted to uncover the social meanings of art. Berger claimed that the real message of Thomas Gainsborough's portrait of *Mr and Mrs Andrews* in the grounds of their country estate was not 'here is a couple in harmony with their surroundings', but 'trespassers keep out'.

The story of Western art until the 20th century is largely about the 'Masterpieces' of great male artists. This is because women have, until recently, been denied the freedom and opportunity to become artists. They were not allowed equal access to art schools and academies. They were distanced from the male-dominated social and political life of their times. It should not be a surprise then that a large part of the art produced by women over the centuries, much of it unsung, has focused on the home.

THOMAS GAINSBOROUGH,
MR AND MRS ANDREWS, C.1748-9
REPRODUCED COURTESY OF
THE TRUSTEES OF THE
NATIONAL GALLERY, LONDON

This is true of the women associated with the first and most popular of modern art movements, the Impressionists. Everyone is familiar with the colourful Impressionist paintings of the social life of the Parisian middle classes in the 1870s: the boulevard scenes of Renoir and Monet, Degas and Manet's depictions of cafe society and the ballet. Less well known are the paintings of Berthe Morisot and Mary Cassatt, even though Morisot was described by one critic, in 1877, as 'the one real Impressionist in this group'. The art of Morisot and Cassatt, and their opportunity to promote it, was limited by conventions surrounding their femininity. They were unable to ask men outside of their family to pose, and their access to the public domain of the male Impressionists was restricted. Most of their paintings, therefore, are of domestic scenes.

In the early 20th century, even a relatively liberated woman artist, Gwen John, felt most comfortable recording the quiet life of the home. Much of her work was of empty interiors, especially her rooms in Rue du Cherche-Midi in Paris. In a letter to the sculptor Rodin, John declared: "I am not myself except in my room."

It is one thing to represent the places and events of everyday life in art, it is quite another to argue that art has any real place or meaning in an everyday context. Indeed, until the arrival of public museums and art galleries in the 18th and 19th centuries, most people's contact with art would have been limited to what could be seen in their local church.

In Britain, the establishment's desire to widen access to art and culture led to the foundation of institutions like the British Museum in 1753, the Royal Academy in 1768, and the National Gallery in 1824. In the early days, though, entry tended to be for the privileged few, such as artists seeking to learn from Old Master paintings. Access increased when wealth generated by the Industrial Revolution led to a growth in the educated middle classes, fuelling an unprecedented demand for culture. By the end of the 19th century, even the poor were encouraged to attend exhibitions at places like the newly opened Whitechapel Art Gallery in London's East End. Art had come to be regarded as a tool for the education and 'moral improvement' of the masses. Advances in technology and increased living standards also meant that ordinary people could, for the first time, bring art into their homes in the form of prints and illustrations.

A hundred years on, though, it seems that, despite a vast and sophisticated

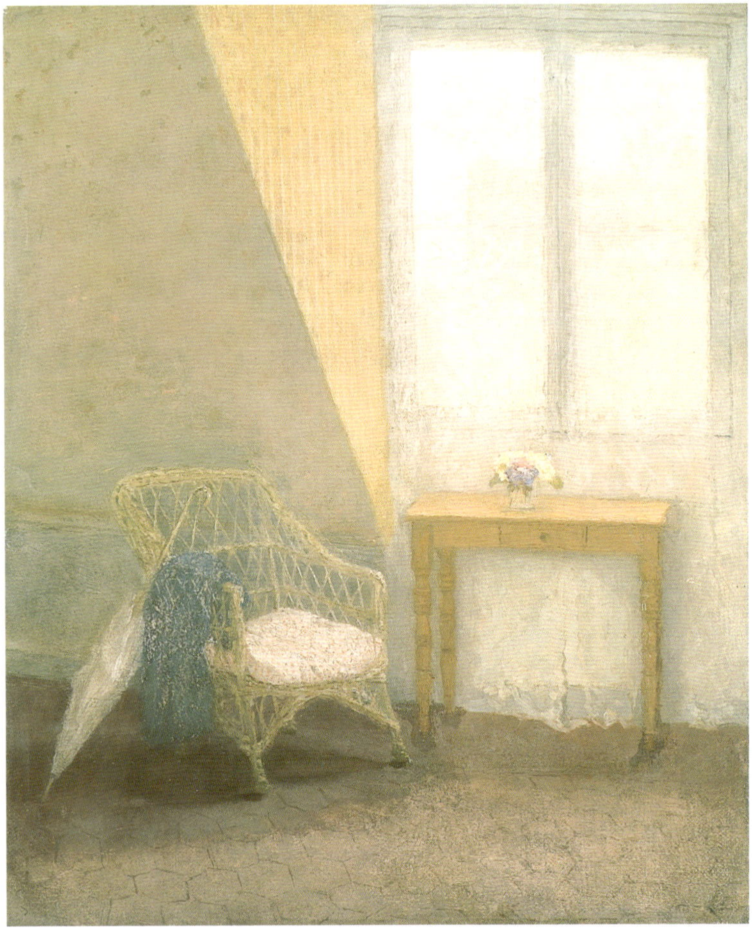

GWEN JOHN, *A CORNER OF THE ARTIST'S ROOM IN PARIS*, 1907-09
COURTESY OF SHEFFIELD CITY ART GALLERIES AND BRIDGEMAN ART LIBRARY, LONDON, © ESTATE OF GWEN JOHN/DACS 1997

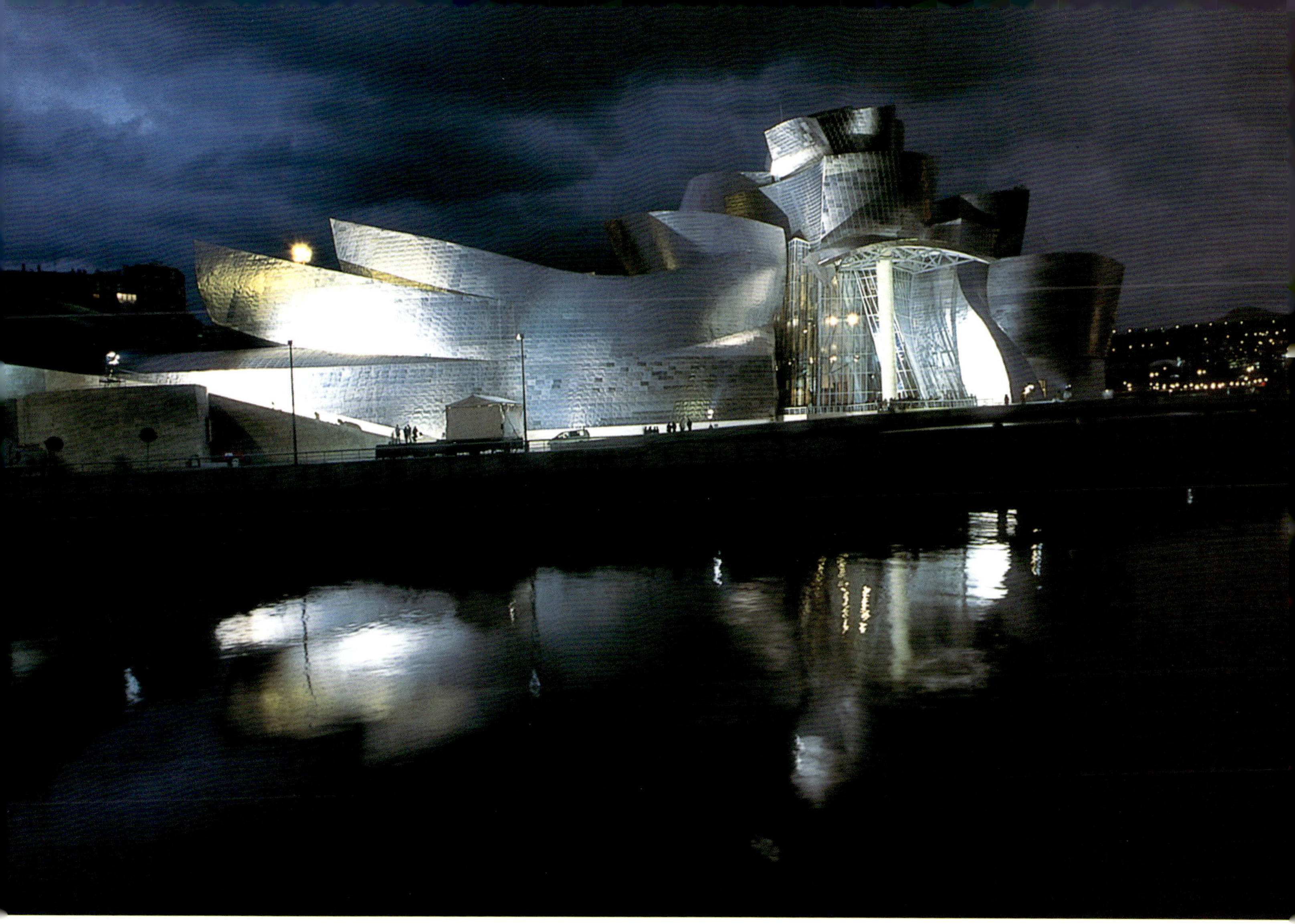

machinery for circulating information and ideas about art – from schools, to television, to free art galleries in many towns and cities – most people today do not really feel 'at home' with the art of their time. The reason for this is twofold. Firstly, the nature of art has changed radically. Indeed, a major concern of 20th-century artists has been to question just what art is, or could be. With new styles and movements following each other in rapid succession it is little wonder that many people feel left behind. Secondly, the specialisation of art – which has led to separate colleges of art, and to a dictionary full of 'isms'- means that it is now seen as a distinct world which has little in common with everyday life.

GUGGENHEIM MUSEUM, BILBAO, 1997
REPRODUCED COURTESY OF
RICHARD BRYANT/ARCHAID

In many people's eyes, the home of art today is the clean white gallery: a shrine to culture, where only the initiated are welcome to worship. This has been the popular image of the modern art gallery since the late 1920s, when the Museum of Modern Art, New York, first opened its doors to the well-to-do culture vultures of uptown Manhattan. In recent years a fresh wave of flamboyant museums of contemporary art have sprung up all over the world. The latest is the breathtaking Guggenheim Museum in Bilbao, Northern Spain. Designed by the architect Frank Gehry, and built at a cost of $100 million, this vast and shining new temple of culture is indeed cathedral-like in the way that it dominates its surroundings.

TAKING ART APART: in which artists find new things to say, and new ways of saying them

If the modern art gallery has acquired an aura of elitism and otherworldliness, though, it could be argued that, materially speaking, art in the 20th Century has in a very real sense come down-to-earth. At the end of the 19th Century, artists' materials were much as they had been for centuries: charcoal for drawing, oil paint and watercolour for painting, and stone and bronze for sculpting. For many people today, these are still what art is, or should be, about. But why so? Scientists in the past hundred years have shown that there are many more ways of getting from A to B than by horse and cart. Artists have discovered that the same holds true in terms of how materials can be used to explore and express ideas.

Amongst the many efforts to radically transform art in the 20th Century, one, in particular, stands out. In 1913 Marcel Duchamp set out to explode the notion that 'art' necessarily referred to a specially crafted object when he mounted a bicycle wheel on a kitchen stool, thus inventing, what he called, the 'ready made'. Duchamp took this idea a step further in 1917 when, under the pseudonym of Richard Mutt, he submitted a urinal to a sculpture exhibition in New York. Although the exhibition was, in theory, open to any artist who could afford the $6 entry fee, the urinal - which Duchamp called *Fountain* - was not shown.

Duchamp recounted the episode in a journal called *The Blind Man*:
"Mr Richard Mutt sent in a fountain. Without discussion this article disappeared and never was exhibited. What were the grounds for refusing Mr Mutt's fountain? 1. Some contended that it was immoral, vulgar. 2. Others, it was plagiarism, a plain piece of plumbing. Now Mr Mutt's fountain is not immoral, that is absurd, no more than a bathtub is immoral. It is a fixture that you see every day. Whether Mr Mutt with his own hands made the fountain or not has no importance. He CHOSE it. He took an ordinary article of life, placed it so that its useful significance disappeared under the new title and point of view - created a new thought for that object. As for plumbing, that is absurd. The only works of art America has given the world are her plumbing and her bridges."

Although it is by no means true that upon hearing of the 'ready made' artists began to throw away their paintbrushes and sculpting chisels, Duchamp's argument that art can be made of anything an artist wants it to be made of has steadily gained acceptance. *Date With An Artist's* Cornelia Parker – who sees Duchamp as 'a hero' – acknowledges the importance of his idea: "he would just take an ordinary object, rename it and say that 'this is just as much a work of art as a Rembrandt', that was a huge revolutionary step in the history of art." Duchamp's major breakthrough was his insistence that what mattered most in art was not the *making* of the object, but the *thinking* behind it. It is a point of view that has made 'conceptual art' possible. "Art is no longer just about technique", says Parker. "It's about implementing your ideas, about finding new ways of saying things that seem appropriate for the way we live now. People take years to achieve technical skills, like drawing and painting. It has taken me years to achieve a way of thinking."

Duchamp had a second major insight which has profoundly influenced how many 20th-century artists have approached their work. "A work of art", said Duchamp, "is only a work of art for a very short period. After twenty years an Impressionist painting has ceased to be an Impressionist painting, because the material, the colour, the paint has darkened so much that it is no more what it first was... After twenty years all works of art are finished; their life is over. It is a condition of contemporary life."

This assertion poses a huge challenge to the romantic notion that art works have an 'eternal' value – a belief summed up in the phrase 'a thing of beauty is a joy forever'. Even our top custodian of Old Master paintings, the National Gallery Director, Neil MacGregor, would recognise some truth in it. In acknowledging that the muddy grey sky in Paolo Veronese's painting *The Vision of Saint Helena* is a pale reflection of what it once was, MacGregor, noted recently that: "A picture like the *Saint Helena,* reminds us that every painting is a dialogue between the artist and his materials. If those materials are unstable or change, then what it communicates will be distorted."

For many 20th Century artists it has been more important to try to give a vivid sense of the 'here and now' than to take pains to ensure that the materials they were using would preserve their vision for posterity.

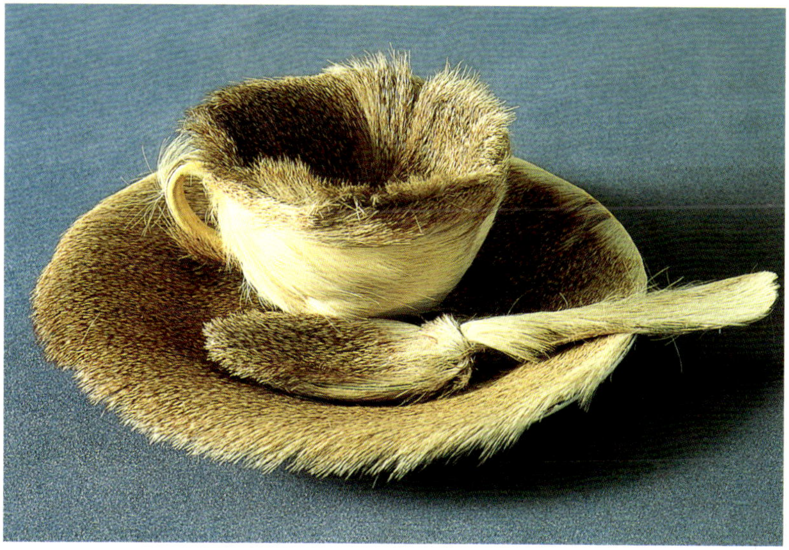

MERET OPPENHEIM, *OBJECT (LUNCHEON IN FUR)*, 1936, REPRODUCED COURTESY OF THE MUSEUM OF MODERN ART, NEW YORK, © DACS 1997

Marcel Duchamp was by no means alone, in the first decades of the 20th century, in trying to redefine the nature and content of art. Pablo Picasso and Georges Braque actually anticipated Duchamp's attempt to make art from the materials of everyday life when, in 1912, they incorporated bric-a-brac, such as newspaper, wallpaper and oilcloth, directly into their Cubist collages. The collage idea – where bits and pieces of materials originally intended for other uses are recycled into art works – has proved popular with many artists since. It is a technique favoured by *Date With An Artist's* Chris Ofili.

In parallel with the political and social upheavals which culminated in the Great War of 1914–18 and in the 1917 Russian Revolution, a succession of artistic movements sought to fundamentally question and re-evaluate just what art was, or could be. In 1909, an Italian group, the Futurists, issued a manifesto insisting that traditional art was dead: "We declare that the world's splendour has been enriched by a new beauty: the beauty of speed. A roaring automobile, which seems to run like a machine gun, is more beautiful than the *Victory of Samothrace* " (a famous antique sculpture). Futurist painters like Severini and Boccioni set out to capture the energy and dynamism of modern city life in vibrant canvases full of movement and colour.

When the glamour of modern machinery was tarnished in the killing fields of the Great War, a group of disillusioned artists and writers based in Zurich, Switzerland, invented Dada: an anarchic, absurd phenomenon which blatantly challenged the discredited culture that had led to the war. Committed to spontaneity and the unexpected, Dada never had a definable method or style. 'Dada', said Tristan Tzara, one of its leaders, 'is a state of mind'. The Dada attitude soon spread from Zurich to other major cultural centres, like Paris and New York. Marcel Duchamp's *Fountain* was a subversive gesture in the true Dada spirit.

After the war, Dada failed to sustain its negative energy and, in Paris in 1924, Surrealism, preaching a positive attitude to the irrational, was born out of its ashes. The Surrealists, including painters such as Salvador Dali and Max Ernst, rejected the humdrum reality of the visible world in favour of the hidden, in their view superior, reality of dreams and of the uncensored imagination. In order to tap into the irrational depths and reproduce the fantastic logic of dreams, the Surrealists experimented with new techniques, such as the bringing together of usually unconnected objects and materials. The results were often startling and uncanny. Meret Oppenheim's *Object* (or *Luncheon in Fur*), a fur-covered cup, saucer and spoon, is an example of how simple domestic objects can be powerfully transformed by this process. The work of *Date With An Artist's* Hadrian Pigott, Nina Saunders and the Chapman brothers owes much to the philosophy and the example of the Surrealists.

At the same time as Dada attempted to dismantle art in the West, a group in Eastern Europe, known as the Constructivists, tried to reconstruct art in the aftermath of the 1917 Russian Revolution. In the new communist society, where the old values no longer appeared relevant, there seemed an opportunity to rethink completely what the role of art should be. Artists like Vladimir Tatlin and Alexander Rodchenko believed that art should serve social aims. Not content to make paintings and sculptures to show in galleries, they saw art as just another form of labour, and they looked for ways to incorporate it directly into the social fabric. For a time, Tatlin worked in a factory, designing clothing, furniture, stoves and other household objects for the workers. By 1924, however, the Communist hierarchy had begun to frown on anything that appeared too free-thinking and experimental, and Constructivism was brought to a halt.

Although each of the pioneering artistic movements of the early 20th Century was short-lived, the attitudes, techniques and ideas developed during this revolutionary period have been taken up by many artists since. Their lasting legacy is that they have altered forever our perception of what art is and can be.

JUST WHAT IS IT THAT MAKES TODAY'S ART SO INTERESTING, SO APPEALING?: in which post-war artists turn the 'low brow' into 'high art'

The generation of artists which emerged after World War II, then, inherited a number of important insights from their predecessors. Amongst other things, they had been shown that modern art should not be bound by age-old conventions; that it could seek to represent unconscious, as well as visible, reality; that it could find inspiration in humble and mass-produced objects and materials; that it could affect the quality and content of everyday life. Above all, perhaps, they had been taught that their aim should be to find new ways to record and reflect what seemed important in the here and now.

As the world left behind the dark years of the War, artists found a confidence and creative energy to take these discoveries further. In Britain and North America an art emerged which wanted to reflect the expanding consumer society and the ideas and images which were being circulated via the cinema, television and advertising. Coming at a time when Prime Minister Harold Macmillan told the British people "you've never had it so good", critic Lawrence Alloway called it "an aesthetics of plenty". It grew into a movement called 'Pop'.

The Pop attitude was already evident by 1956, in the exhibition *This Is Tomorrow*, at the Whitechapel Art Gallery. Organised by the forward-thinking Independent Group, *This Is Tomorrow* consisted of twelve collaboratively designed environments. Painter Richard Hamilton, sculptor John McHale, and architect John Voelcker created *The Fun House*, a brash, noisy space filled with cinema projections, a juke box, and a science fiction chamber. On display outside were a life-sized cut-out of Marilyn Monroe and a giant beer bottle. The exhibition was opened by Robby the Robot, hero of the popular sci-fi film *The Forbidden Planet*.

This Is Tomorrow showed that the latest generation of artists were not interested in the conventional subject-matter of 'high art'; they wanted to engage directly with the busy flow of media images which surrounded them. "My life as an artist having been built on the idea that painters responded to nature", recalls Hamilton, "it was interesting to find that that wasn't what I was doing. I was responding to pictures in magazines, or comics or cinema or whatever. I think this is the thing that unites people labelled 'Pop artists'."

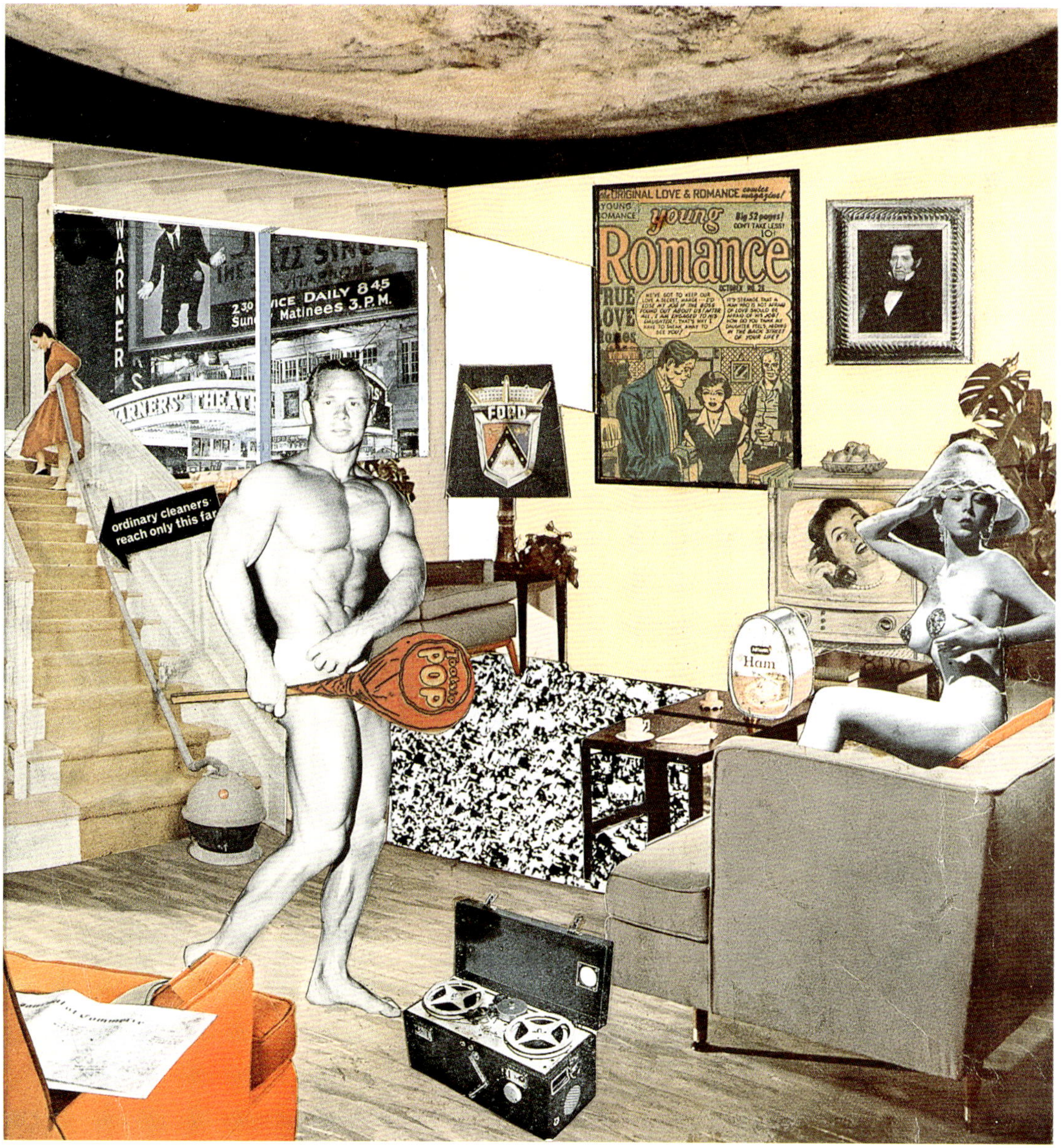

RICHARD HAMILTON, *JUST WHAT IS IT THAT MAKES TODAY'S HOMES SO INTERESTING, SO APPEALING?*, 1956, REPRODUCED COURTESY OF KUNSTHALLE TÜBINGEN, GERMANY, © RICHARD HAMILTON 1997, ALL RIGHTS RESERVED DACS

For the catalogue and poster of This Is Tomorrow, Richard Hamilton produced one of the best-known works of British Pop. Collaged together from pictures cut out of magazines, *Just what is it that makes today's homes so different, so appealing?* shows a living-room filled with all the latest mod cons. Closer inspection reveals that the ceiling is an image of the earth taken from outer space and that the patterned rug is really an aerial photograph of a crowded beach. A far cry from traditional depictions of a domestic interior, there was nothing precious or exclusive about this new way of picturing the home. Hamilton declared, in 1957, that Pop art should be: "Popular (for a mass audience), Transient (short-term), Expendable (easily forgotten), Low cost, Mass produced, Young (aimed at youth), Witty, Sexy, Gimmicky, Glamorous, Big Business". This formula seems as relevant to the, so-called, Young British Artists of today as it was for their equivalents of 40 years ago.

By the beginning of the 1960s, a fresh wave of young Pop artists had emerged from London's Royal College of Art. It included painters, such as Peter Blake and David Hockney, who showed an interest in a new breed of hero, the pop or film star. Hockney's 1961 painting *We 2 Boys Together Clinging*, is a disguised tribute to his idol Cliff Richard. It was partly inspired by a newspaper headline 'Two Boys Cling to Cliff All Night', which Hockney got very excited about – though the headline actually referred to a climbing accident. At around the same time, Peter Blake used pictures of Elvis Presley in his collage *Got a Girl*, 1960–1. Across the Atlantic, Andy Warhol was pursuing a similar interest. His famous screen-prints of pop-culture icons like Marilyn Monroe, Elizabeth Taylor and Elvis were made during the same period. It was perhaps predictable, if ironic, that these glamorous portraits of glamorous people would make star-struck Warhol a celebrity in his own right.

A fascination with celebrity and the way in which it is fuelled by the media continues to inspire artists. *Date With an Artist's* Jessica Voorsanger is one of the latest exponents of this typically late 20th-century genre of star-based art.

Pop art's recycling of subject-matter from existing, usually mass-produced, sources – such as images of movie stars from magazines – echoed Marcel Duchamp's recycling of objects into 'ready mades'. In both cases the traditional notion that a work of art should be entirely new and original was ignored. For most Pop artists, though, the primary material continued to be paint. Elsewhere in Europe, a version of Pop art grew up that was closer in both spirit and substance to the art of Duchamp. In 1960 French critic, Pierre Restany, invented the term *Le Nouveau Réalisme* (New Realism) to describe an art which aimed to represent reality as rawly and directly as possible. Like Pop, New Realism was inspired by popular culture, technology and the urban environment. Like Pop too, it liked to recycle already existing things.

When concrete objects, rather than images, were brought together to make surprising new configurations the term *assemblage*, not collage, was preferred. One such assemblage is *Condition of Woman I*, by New Realist artist Arman. It consists of a traditional carved wooden pedestal, from Arman's father's antique shop, on which is placed a glass box full of discarded objects found in his first wife's bathroom. Arman also made several *poubelles* (dustbin works) based on rubbish provided by his friends. A form of modern-day portraiture, these poubelles played on the idea that we are what we consume. Like Arman, *Date With An Artist's* Hadrian Pigott and Nina Saunders often make use of assemblage. Where Arman seemed obsessed with household rubbish, Pigott's works, particularly his soap pieces, deal with the other side of the coin: our obsession with hygiene.

FROM BRICKS TO HOUSES TO IDEAL HOMES: a DIY guide to contemporary art

Whilst Pop and New Realist artists were using objects and images from everyday life in a symbolic way, to make people think about contemporary reality, a group known as the Minimalists were interested in the more basic character of everyday materials. Minimalism, which emerged from the United States in the mid 1960s, believed that the aim of art should be to stimulate experience, not thought. Minimalist artists, like Carl Andre and Donald Judd, tried to create a pure art that would eliminate ideas and just make people aware of the raw physical presence of things, and of their bodies in relation to those things. To achieve this it was necessary that the things chosen should trigger as few thoughts and associations as possible, hence the name Minimalism. Minimalist sculptures usually consisted of identical units of industrial materials, such as various kinds of bricks and metals, arranged in very basic patterns. "My work is about the fundamental innocence of matter," said Carl Andre. "I don't start with a concept or a drawing. I start with a set of physical realities which I order in a way that I find satisfying to me."

The public, which had warmed to Pop, felt uncomfortable with Minimalism. Although Minimalist sculpture was made from things that were as familiar as the things that went into Pop art, there was puzzlement and suspicion that it didn't seem to be about anything. After the Tate Gallery purchased Carl Andre's *Equivalent VIII* (popularly known as 'the bricks') in 1972 there was a public outcry. Some critics and journalists complained that Minimalism was too simple to be art. They failed to get the point. If Minimalism was trying to say anything it was that there is too much meaning in the world, too much visual information clamouring to be interpreted. Art, said the Minimalists, should not create more meaning. Instead it should try to refocus our attention on a very basic question that we seemed to be losing sight of: what it feels like to be.

In trying to rid art of ideas by emphasising the basic physical truth of materials, the Minimalists were swimming against the tide. A more widespread tendency in the late 1960s and early 70s was the tendency away from specific materials and towards ideas. It was during this period that people first started talking about 'conceptual art'.

Conceptual art, a blanket term covering a huge range of activity, could, in fact, take any form. With conceptual art the form, or the material, was not the primary consideration. What came first was the idea.

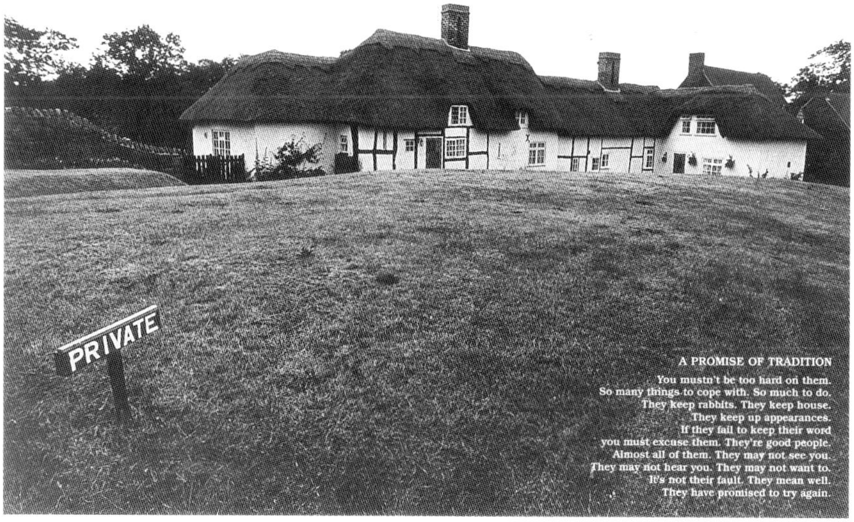

VICTOR BURGIN,
A PROMISE OF TRADITION, 1976,
REPRODUCED COURTESY
OF THE ARTIST

Conceptual art in the late 60s was closely identified with the anti-establishment politics of the time. It was an era when student revolts threatened to topple governments in Europe and when Civil Rights and Anti-Vietnam campaigns set a generation of young people in the United States against its political masters. Conceptual artists rebelled against the luxury status of art by inventing forms of art that wealthy collectors either couldn't, or wouldn't want to buy. The art might consist of photographic or written documentation; of sculpture made of low-value, sometimes perishable materials; or even of the artist's own actions. Unlike Pop art, which was often as seductive as the advertising imagery that inspired it, conceptual art was seldom beautiful in any conventional sense. Beauty was, in fact, distrusted as something that might make the work more marketable, or draw attention away from the idea, or message, and onto the form which contained it.

A leading British conceptual artist, Victor Burgin, explaining why much of his art consisted of words and photographs, recalled the general feeling that: "There were enough paintings and sculptures silting up the basements of museums all over the world – why produce more? It was ecologically unsound: a form of pollution... We wanted an art of pure information that didn't use up materials, wasn't costly and wasn't wasteful." Burgin chose photography because he considered it more down-to-earth and democratic than, say, painting. It was something that everyone could feel at home with. "You don't need to have been to art school for three years to read a photograph", he said. *A Promise of Tradition*, from the series *UK 76*, is typical of Burgin's work from this period. Like much Pop art, it is made up of elements taken from, or mimicking, the language of advertising. Where Pop tended to celebrate its sources, however, conceptual art aimed to subvert. In its implied attack on the ruling classes, and its refusal of the pleasurable attributes expected of an art work – colour, for example, or surface texture – *A Promise of Tradition* could be seen as modern art's revenge on Gainsborough's *Mr and Mrs Andrews*.

Victor Burgin used conceptual art to satirise the home life of Britain's wealthy. At the same time, a young artist called Gordon Matta-Clarke used conceptual art in a very different way to make a statement about the living conditions of America's urban poor. In 1976 Matta-Clarke, who trained as an architect, was invited to participate in an exhibition called *Idea as Model* at New York's Institute of Architecture and Urbanism. He made his contribution at 3 am on the day before the exhibition opened. Armed with a borrowed air rifle, he entered the Institute's exhibition space and blew out all the windows. He then covered up the holes with photographs of a new housing block in the South Bronx, whose windows had been smashed by the occupants.

For a brief moment, architecture's inner-sanctum was subjected to the same anarchy and violence as a South Bronx tenement. By blasting away the windows, Matta-Clarke suddenly connected the Institute in well-to-do downtown Manhattan to the poverty-stricken neighbourhoods of New York's urban fringe. "The very real nature of my work with buildings takes issue with the attitude of modern architecture, which has failed to question or re-examine the quality of life being served", he said. As with Duchamp's *Fountain* sixty years earlier, the New York public never got to see Matta-Clarke's conceptual exhibit. The photographs were removed and the broken glass was replaced before the exhibition opened.

Window Blow-Out illustrates an important characteristic of much conceptual art: an emphasis on the process by which the work is made, not just on the final product. Process was crucial to the activity that Matta-Clarke was more generally known for: *anarchitecture*. A cross between sculpture, architecture and demolition, anarchitecture used whole buildings for its raw material. Just as a stone-carver chips away excess material to reveal the form within, so Matta-Clarke would hack his way through the walls, ceilings and floors of abandoned houses and apartment blocks. *Splitting*, 1964, for example, consisted of a house which had been cut right through: from the roof deep into the foundations, making one half of the dwelling tilt precariously away from the other. Each visitor faced a similar perilous and exhilarating experience to that which Matta-Clarke had undergone in making the work. In Matta-Clarke's anarchitectural works, which he called *non-uments*, the safety that the home usually represents was literally undermined. When you entered a non-ument, neither the roof over your head, nor the ground beneath your feet offered comfort or security.

Since the 1960s the home and domestic life have continued to feature regularly in contemporary art. In Britain, women artists, in particular, have made memorable art works around house-related ideas. Unlike Gwen John in the early years of the 20th Century, artists like Cornelia Parker and Rachel Whiteread have not been satisfied to paint pictures of their living rooms. In keeping with our post-feminist times they have chosen to make a more assertive mark on the world.

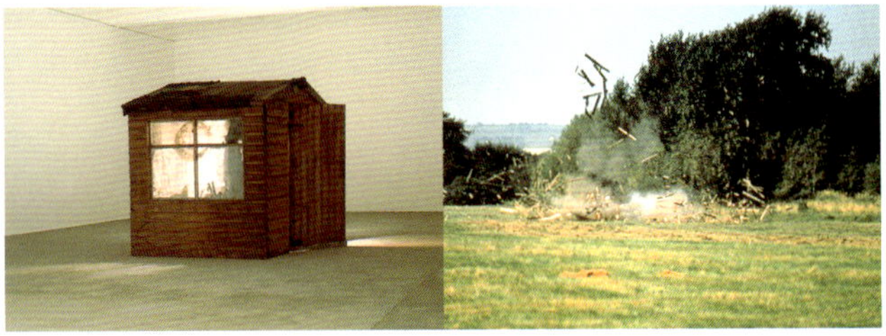

Cornelia Parker's *Cold, Dark Matter: An Exploded View*, 1991, consisted of a garden shed and its contents which were exhibited, intact, at London's Chisenhale Gallery. The shed was then transported to Banbury where it was blown up by the British Army. The fragments were collected and taken back to the gallery, where they were suspended on metal wire around a single light bulb. The overall impression of the final installation was not of an explosion frozen in time, but of a very deliberate formal arrangement centred on a light bulb, suggesting a bizarre and beautiful miniature solar system. The work was inspired by the idea of bringing about a collision between two very different kinds of British institution: a normally safe and cosy institution, the garden shed, and a massive and formidable institution, the army.

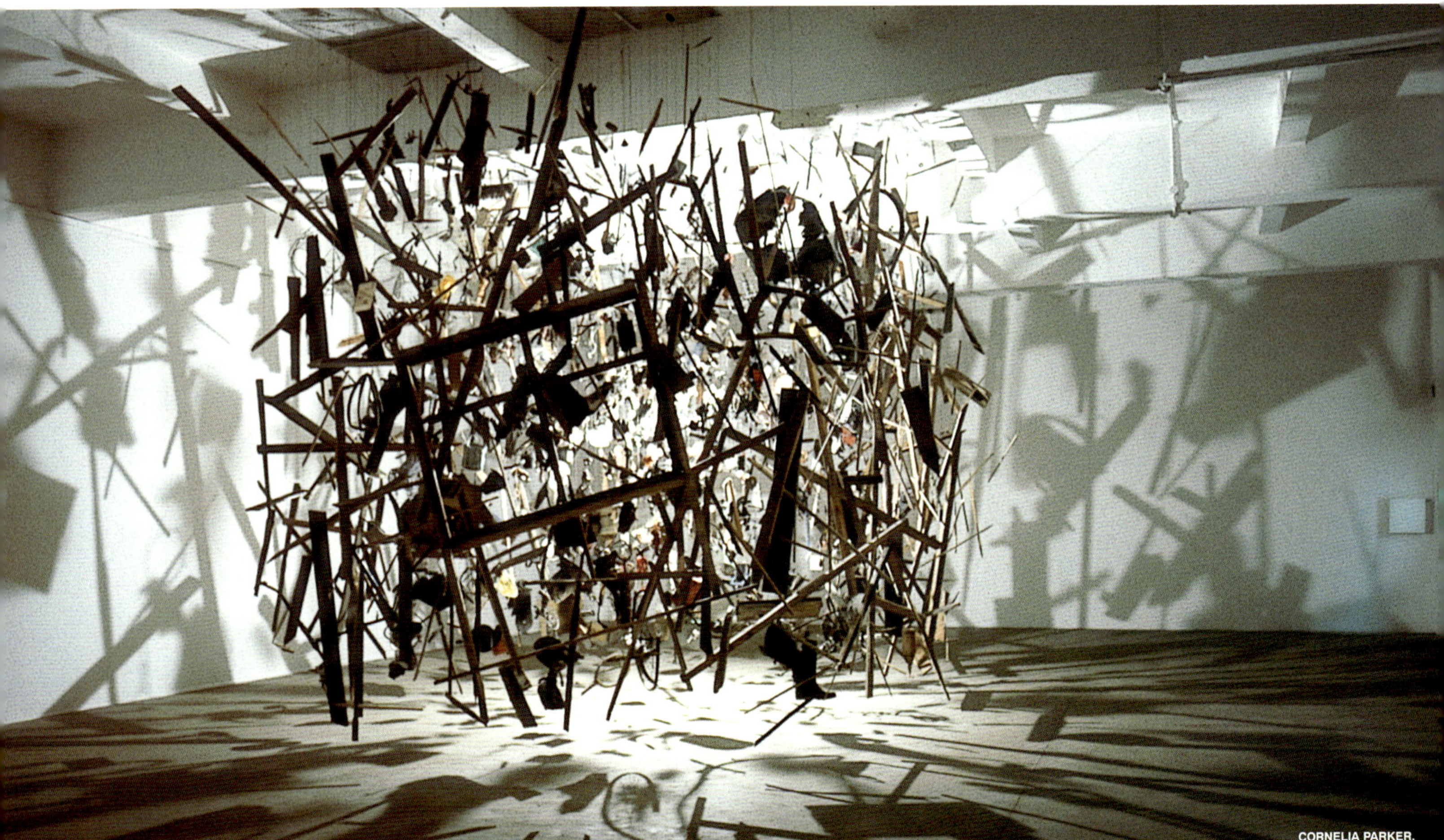

CORNELIA PARKER, *COLD, DARK MATTER: AN EXPLODED VIEW*, 1991, COURTESY OF THE ARTIST AND HUGO GLENDINNING

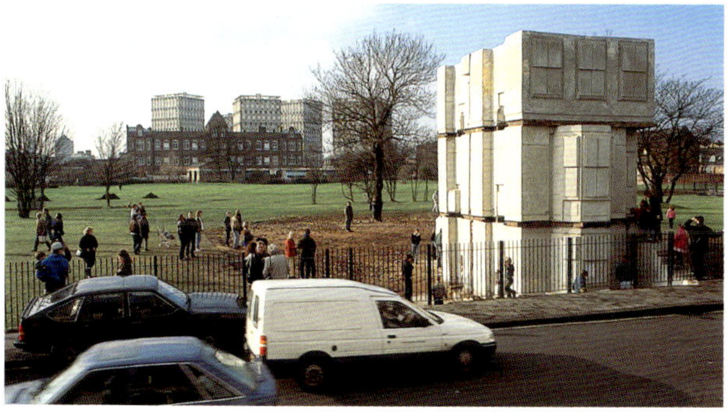

RACHEL WHITEREAD, *HOUSE*,
OCTOBER 1993 - JANUARY 94,
COMMISSIONED BY ARTANGEL

As a piece of 1990s conceptual art, Parker's *Cold, Dark Matter* had significant features in common with Gordon Matta-Clarke's *Window Blow-Out*. In both cases, an act of violence against property was involved in the making of the work. In both cases the process by which the work was created was as important as the final form of the work itself. What, perhaps, distinguishes Parker's work – and indeed most of today's conceptual art – from the art of Matta-Clarke and his contemporaries is the lack of a political point of view. Whilst today's conceptual artists continue to try and provoke thoughts, they are not, on the whole, concerned to make statements or convey specific messages.

Probably the most haunting of all recent projects which have engaged with ideas of domesticity, was Rachel Whiteread's *House*. Number 193 Grove Road in the East End of London, the last remaining dwelling in a Victorian terrace, was brimming with meanings and memories which Whiteread was able to unlock through a bold act of transformation. The formal idea behind the work was simple: to fill a house with liquid concrete and then strip away the mould – that is, the house itself, bricks, doors, windows and all – leaving, in effect, the negative of a house. Despite its size and solidity, *House* had quite a ghostly, funereal presence. It seemed to connect with a sense of mourning at the passing away of a popular kind of housing. At once a closed architectural form and an open memorial, *House* was able to absorb all the individual thoughts, feelings and memories that the visiting public wished to project onto it.

Completed in late October 1993, *House* provoked complex, sometimes extreme, reactions all the way from the streets of Bow to the House of Commons. By the time it was demolished less than three months later on 11 January 1994, House had been seen by an estimated 100,000 people and had become a focus of media attention around the world. The decision to demolish *House* was made by Bow Council, on 23 November 1993. Later that day, Rachel Whiteread became the first woman to win the coveted Turner Prize.

Parker and Whiteread have shown that in the 1990s art about domestic themes can take on spectacular and imposing forms. A recent work by Donald Rodney, *In the House of My Father*, offered a reminder that small can be equally as beautiful and affecting. Rodney has been afflicted since childhood by sickle-cell anaemia, a disease which affects people of African and Caribbean origin. The pain which has blighted his life, has also provided him with the raw material, sometimes literally, for his art. *In the House of My Father* is a tiny house made of skin taken from the artist's thigh during one of his many operations. Held together by pins, this incredibly delicate structure is an image of suffering and vulnerability as well as of belonging. It is also a poignant memorial to the artist's recently deceased father, Harold George Rodney, who left his Caribbean home in 1958 to come to England in search of 'the land of milk and honey'.

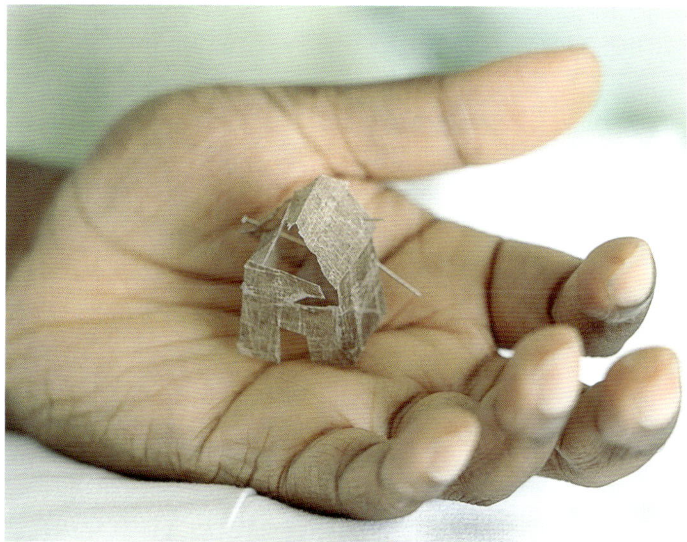

DONALD RODNEY, *IN THE HOUSE OF MY FATHER*, 1997, COURTESY OF THE SOUTH LONDON GALLERY

As well as making art about homes, often using materials found in homes, there have been a number of recent occasions, prior to *Date With An Artist*, where artists have worked directly in people's home environments. In 1986, in a bold experiment called *Chambres d'Amis: a museum ventures out*, fifty citizens of the Belgian town of Ghent put their homes at the disposal of fifty artists. The artists' task was "to transform these spaces – within the limits imposed by the occupants – into art". The curator, Jan Hoet, saw the project as a way of 'cutting the museum to pieces and scattering it all over town.' "The beauty of *Chambres d'Amis* ", said Hoet, "is that it shows how remoteness can be suddenly quite near, how it can live in anybody's house like a friendly, yet mysterious intruder, where it does not occupy space but, on the contrary, creates more space."

The homes were not just temporary art galleries, they were also the inspiration for the artists' ideas. American artist Dan Graham chose to work with the space surrounding his adopted house. He made a *Children's Pavilion*, in which it was impossible for grown-ups to stand, in the middle of the path connecting the back and front of the house. It allowed children, who are often pushed to one side, to take their place in the centre. Joseph Kosuth responded to his host's profession. He copied onto the walls of a neurologist's home passages from Sigmund Freud's treatise on lapses in speech. He then covered the words with tape, so that they could be seen but not read. Hovering between legibility and illegibility, they tried to say something but were incomprehensible, like dreams perhaps, or a deranged human mind. Heike Pallanca favoured a more evocative approach. In the recesses of an upstairs room she lit two candles. Visitors entering the room heard the violent rustling of the wind, conveyed through a tape recorder, but the flames burned-on, undisturbed. The French artist Daniel Buren, in what Hoet called, "an almost megalomaniac *tour de force* ", decided to turn the idea of the exhibition on its head. He relocated his *Chambre d'Amis*, back in the museum!

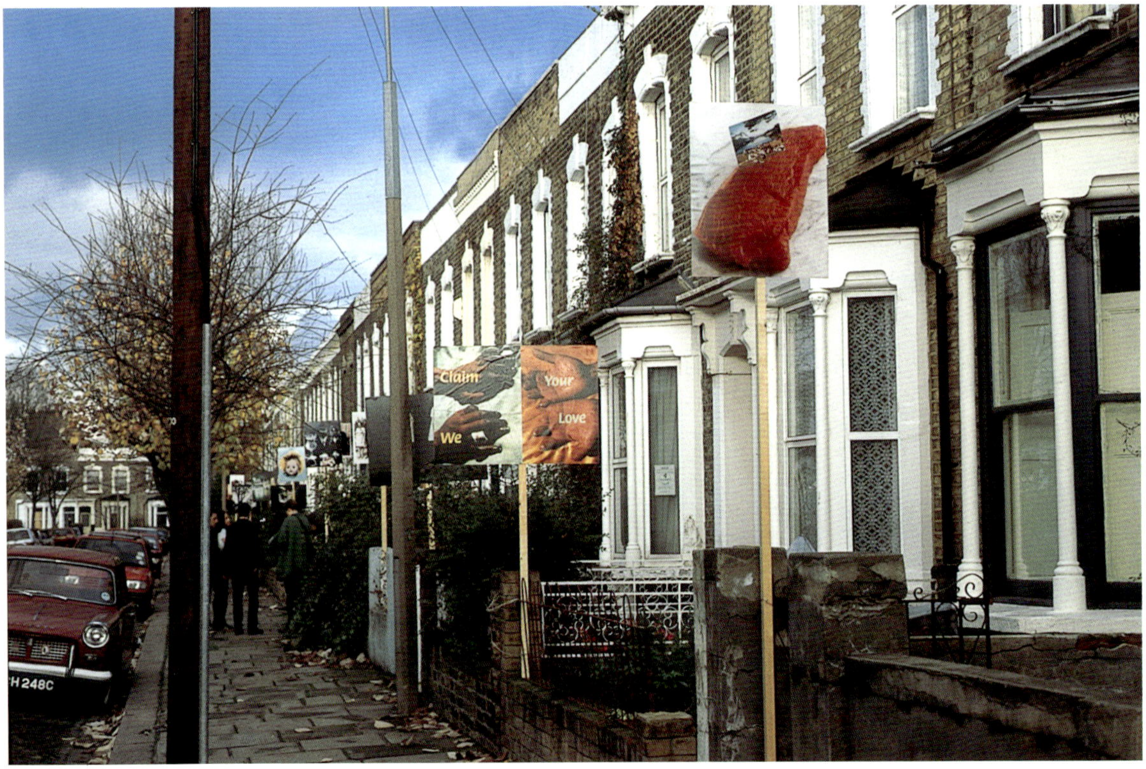

FAT, *HOME IDEALS*, HELD IN THEBERTON STREET, ISLINGTON, 1997, COURTESY OF FAT

In a 1992 project, *At Home with the Collection*, Simon Grennan and Christopher Sperandio – who, like the Chapman brothers, prefer to work as a team – found another way to bring art into people's homes. They invited the staff of the Lakeside Museum of the Arts and Sciences in Illinois – everyone from the Director to the Receptionist – to choose an object from the Museum's collection and take it home with them. Photographs taken of the objects carefully placed in the participants' houses then formed an exhibition back at the museum. The results were sometimes surprising. One person placed an antique Native American carving next to a Pepsi bottle in an otherwise empty fridge. The point of the exercise was to see what would happen if the rules governing the display of these objects were suspended for a while. Though charged with the responsibility for preserving and keeping objects alive, museums sometimes have the feeling of mausoleums: dead places. It was hoped that, by allowing staff to take them home, the objects would gain a new lease of life in the affections of the borrowers and in the context of a new, living environment.

More recently, in June 1997, a group of artists called FAT (Fashion, Architecture, Taste) worked with the residents of a London street to make art works to display outside their houses. Using the familiar estate agents' sign to explore the lifestyles and aspirations of a whole neighbourhood, *Home Ideals* turned a whole street into a gallery. The residents were initially presented with a catalogue containing images produced by each of the participating artists and were invited to choose one which they felt reflected their own tastes and desires. They then teamed up with the artist who had made their preferred image to create a second, more personal, art work. Both images were then photographically enlarged and displayed in their front gardens on either side of a For Sale sign.

Whilst each of the projects described above succeeded in building bridges between art and everyday life, they were limited in the number of people they could reach. Modern-day technology, though, allows artists to make works which can be experienced in millions of people's homes at once, through television, or via the Internet. From the earliest days of television, in the 1930s, programmes have been made *about* art. Since the late 1960s, however, there have been occasions when artists have made art works specifically *for* television. Some of these have played on the fact that the viewer would be consuming the work in their sitting-room at home.

In 1969, a German television station broadcast Jan Dibbets' *TV as a Fire Place*, which, as its name suggests, created the illusion of a coal fire burning away in the corner of the room. During the Edinburgh Festival in 1971 Scottish Television broadcast ten 'interruptions' by the artist David Hall. They were called interruptions because they appeared between programmes without introduction or explanation. One of them showed a tap running with water which gradually filled the whole screen. Once the TV set was full, the water began to drain away noisily at an angle from the top-left corner of the screen, offering a witty reminder that, far from providing a transparent window on the world, TV relies heavily on tricks and illusions

Television continues to create opportunities for artists. In October 1997, Jake and Dinos Chapman made a television art work for a Channel 4 series called *TV Sculpture*. More recently still, whilst *Date with An Artist* was being filmed, Nina Saunders was commissioned by a cosmetics company to make a new art work in the form of a thirty-second TV commercial. If Pop art in the 1960s narrowed the gap between advertising and art, it seems that Oil of Ulay's new campaign may have eliminated it altogether.

Art today bears meaning in ways that were not traditionally thought relevant. Every aspect of a work is now open to interpretation. Significance may be looked for equally in the image depicted, in the title of the work, or in words used within the work itself. The style of the work, the materials and objects used, and where they come from, can all be important. The process by which the work was made, who helped to make it, and the location at which it is eventually seen or experienced are also factors to be considered. Some people may feel uncomfortable at the idea that each work of art today can be looked at from a range of different angles: that there is no one correct point of view. It would be better to see this as a challenge. Those who feel confused by contemporary art often start by asking: 'what does it mean?'. It is more helpful to ask: 'in what ways can this be meaningful for me?'. As with most aspects of life in the late 20th Century, there are no certain answers. Each viewer must discover for his or herself a way of looking at art that makes sense in terms of their own experience of the world. You only really feel 'at home' with art when you can stop worrying about 'the right interpretation' and find pleasure in the work, for whatever reasons.

DATE 1: CORNELIA PARKER MEETS REBECCA STEPHENS

Cornelia Parker made headlines with her 1995 exhibition, *The Maybe*, at London's Serpentine Gallery. *The Maybe* consisted of actress Tilda Swinton lying motionless in a glass case for a whole week, surrounded by objects - like Churchill's cigar stub and Queen Victoria's stocking - which were only significant because of the famous people who once owned them. In her 1989 work, *Matter and What it Means*, Cornelia memorably captured her interest in the relationship between objects and ideas. She suspended hundreds of battered coins, which had been run over by a train, from the ceiling to make an image of two figures lying side by side. Using valueless money to create something new and surprising is typical of her way of working. "I often take things at a point where they're starting to loose their meaning and try to resurrect a meaning, but not necessarily the original one", she says.

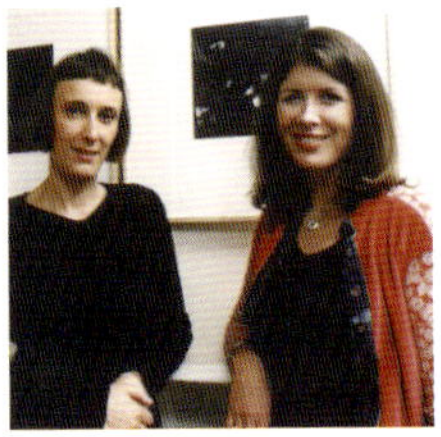

Cornelia chose the first British woman to climb Mount Everest, Rebecca Stephens, for her date. "I wanted to work with someone who was a traveller or explorer", she explained. "Somebody who is doing something quite similar to me; who is out in the world and inquiring into it in a particular kind of way." It was also an attraction of opposites: Cornelia hoped that meeting an intrepid mountaineer might help her to overcome a 'terrible fear of heights'.

Cornelia is not the sort of artist who likes to lock herself away in a garret. "I think my being an artist is, in a way, an excuse to be nosy", she says. "I'm always out and about finding materials and meeting all kinds of people: mountaineers, astronauts, the British Army. I make a lot of work in response to what other people can help me do."

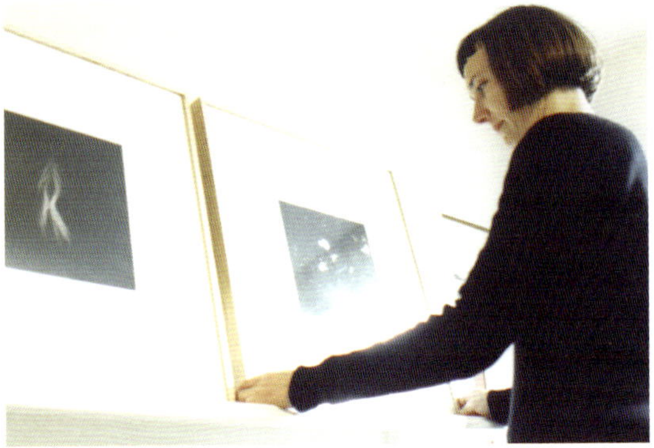

"On my journeys I'm always picking up souvenirs; portable things like feathers from Freud's pillow or dust from his blanket. What I like about these little bits of debris, things like naval fluff and feathers that fall out of pillows, is that they're things that get swept away; they're somehow not monumental. St Paul's Cathedral is monumental, climbing Everest is monumental, but what I'm interested in is the unsung stuff."

Rebecca Stephens found the idea of a date with a contemporary artist intriguing: "I'm fascinated by modern art", she said, "but I'm often along with the masses in thinking, 'is this really art?' I'll be fascinated to talk to Cornelia, just to get a bit more insight into what its all about."

Cornelia took Rebecca along to St Paul's in search of inspiration.

She chose the Cathedral because: "In my old encyclopaedia they used St Paul's to measure the natural world. They would place St Paul's beside Everest, or at the bottom of the deepest ocean. To me it's the equivalent of Everest in London." The famous Whispering Gallery and, in particular, the layers of dust that had gathered there over the ages began to trigger ideas.

Once the germ of an idea is sown, the question for a conceptual artist like Cornelia Parker is how to give it form. "Nowadays, art's not just about technical skill its not about craft", she says. "Its about implementing your ideas, and about finding new ways of saying things that seem appropriate. If my skill is, perhaps, only to do with recognising value in things that people might not otherwise notice, then that's a skill in its own right."

She decided to transform the dust she had gathered into two works. The first, a pair of ear plugs made from compacted St Paul's fluff, typifies her quirky way of turning concepts on their head. "I like the idea of stopping up your ears with something from the Whispering Gallery", she explained. The second work was of a pair of 'photograms': images made by placing objects close to a light source, which fixes the magnified shadow onto light-sensitive paper. One is an image of a tiny speck of dust blown up to unrecognisable proportions. Its companion piece is a beautiful photogram of a feather taken from Rebecca's climbing jacket. The first had spent aeons on the top of St Paul's, the second accompanied Rebecca, fleetingly, to the top of Everest.

Rebecca was impressed by what her date had conjured up from the most unlikely materials. "I just loved what she created", she enthused. "It makes you think from a different angle. I'm already finding that I'm looking at things in a new way. A little feather that comes out of the sofa, or a staple on the floor, I'm saying 'now what could I do with this?' I like that."

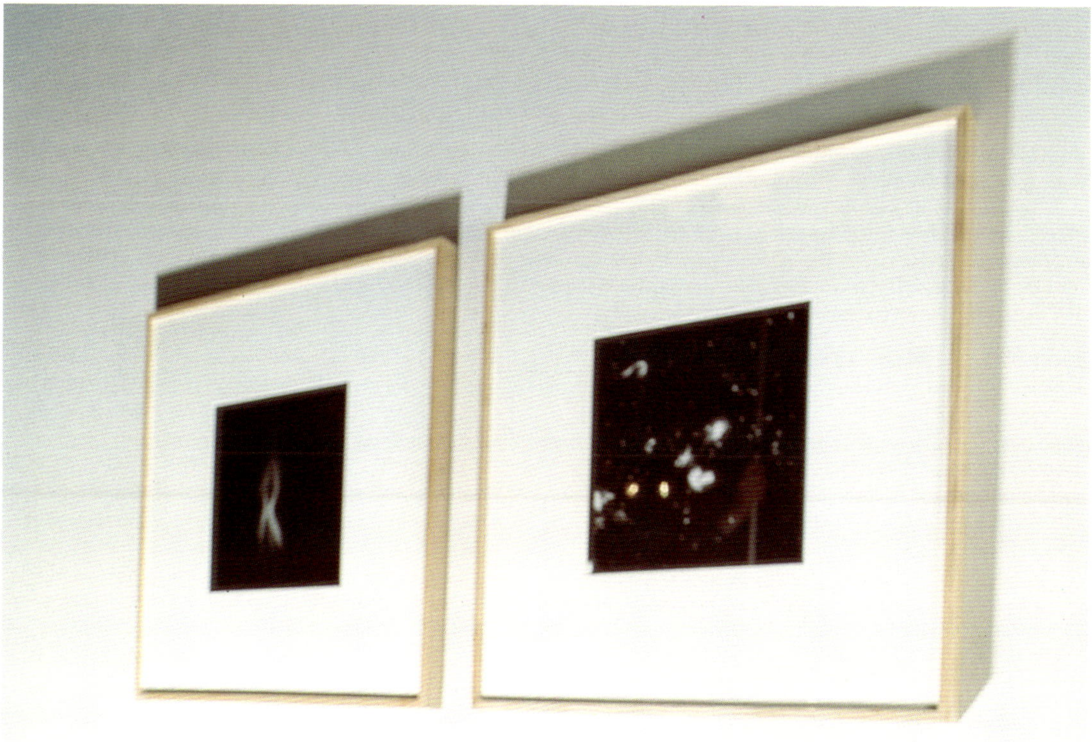

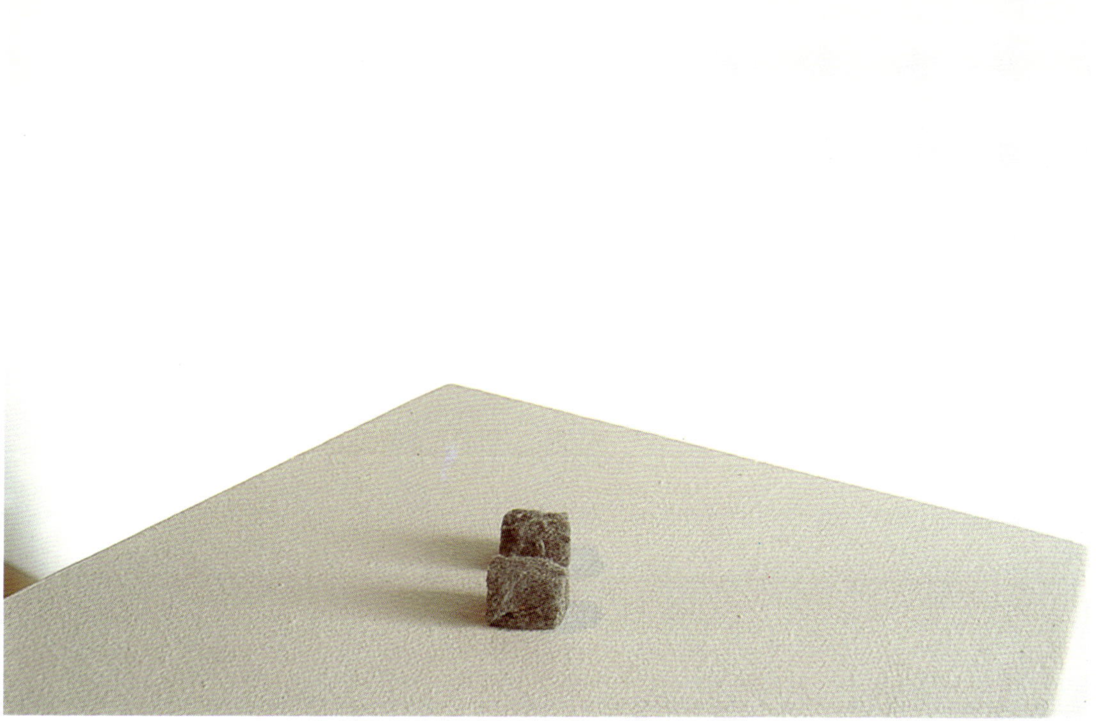

DATE 2: ANDREW GIFFORD MEETS DAVE ALLAN

Andrew Gifford's art is concerned with the changing effects of light and atmosphere. His paintings, usually industrial landscapes painted on site, are influenced by J.M.W. Turner. At the dawning of the industrial age, Turner's eye was powerfully drawn to the effects of steam and smog on the landscape. Although most late 20th-century eyes are wary of what we now regard as pollution, Andrew finds the hazy, chemical-drenched atmosphere of his native Middlesbrough strangely compelling: "A lot of people come up to me when I'm working and ask 'why are you painting the Tees with all that industry in the background? Why don't you go and paint somewhere nice?' Hopefully, the finished painting will help them to see a beauty that perhaps they weren't aware of before."

The flip side of Andrew's art seeks to simulate the vivid experience of light and atmosphere through light-box installations whose colours and intensities mirror those of the external landscape. "I make light installations because light really makes people look at it", says Andrew, "if you're in a crowded pub, people will stare at the TV screen even though the sound's turned down and there's a quiz show on. It's a natural attraction."

Andrew wanted to make work for a fellow Teesider, someone similar to himself: "a young bloke who loves football. Someone I can have a laugh with and relate to." Local knowledge would make him an apt critic: "He'll know the area so he'll be able to tell me whether I've got it right. It's really good to talk to people who don't know much about art because they've got nothing arty to say, just the truth. What's the point in talking to experts when you know what they'll say about your stuff anyway."

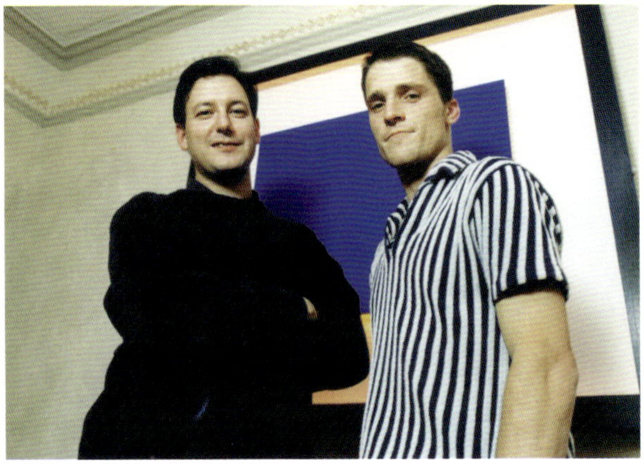

Dave Allan, the Public Relations manager at Middlesbrough FC was Andrew's date. Dave shares Andrew's passions for football and for the industrial scenery of Teeside. "If you see it at the wrong time of day, with the pipes belching, it doesn't look so good", admits Dave, "but at night it can look fantastic, like Blackpool illuminations". As a fan of Salvador Dali's style of art, however, it was not certain that Dave would take to Andrew's landscape approach. "I don't like anything too traditional", Dave declared, before their first meeting. "I love the countryside, but I wouldn't put a country scene up on my wall."

After a day spent looking at Andrew's work and visiting local haunts together, though – including Andrew's favourite spot along the Tees and the beach at Saltburn where Dave walks his dog – Dave was clearly impressed by Andrew's ability and enthusiasm. "I think his work's fantastic", he said. "I was worried when he started talking about landscapes, but that combination of the countryside and industrial backdrops is superb. The best bit of the day was at Saltburn, where Andrew was really buzzing. He was keen to get cracking there and then".

The very next day, in fact, Andrew was back on Saltburn beach with his paints and canvas. He decided, though, that he would make Dave a series of three distant views of Middlesbrough across the Tees: the same view painted at different times of the day – morning, afternoon, and evening – each with their own particular conditions of atmosphere and light. Andrew spent four days painting on site, moving from one canvas to the next as the light changed. He works very quickly, layering up translucent glazes of paint in order to build a rich surface which almost glows like the landscape itself. He then spent a further week in his London studio working the paintings up to their final state. "When I go away from the place", says Andrew, "memory comes into it a bit more and then it becomes a kind of concentrated vision."

Andrew hung the finished paintings over Dave's bed, "so that he'll wake up every morning to beautiful Middlesbrough". He had also prepared a surprise: a vivid blue light installation for the wall opposite. Dave, who was totally unaware of this aspect of Andrew's art was stunned by it. "It threw me at first", he said, "but its fantastic, like a psychedelic trip." Andrew explained that these back-lit installations of perspex and pigment were another means of exploring his fascination with light.

Dave was thoroughly impressed by the effort and talent that Andrew had put into the project. He recognised, too, the heavy sacrifice that Andrew had made for his art. "You have been working hard haven't you", he acknowledged, "no wonder you don't have time for the Boro any more."

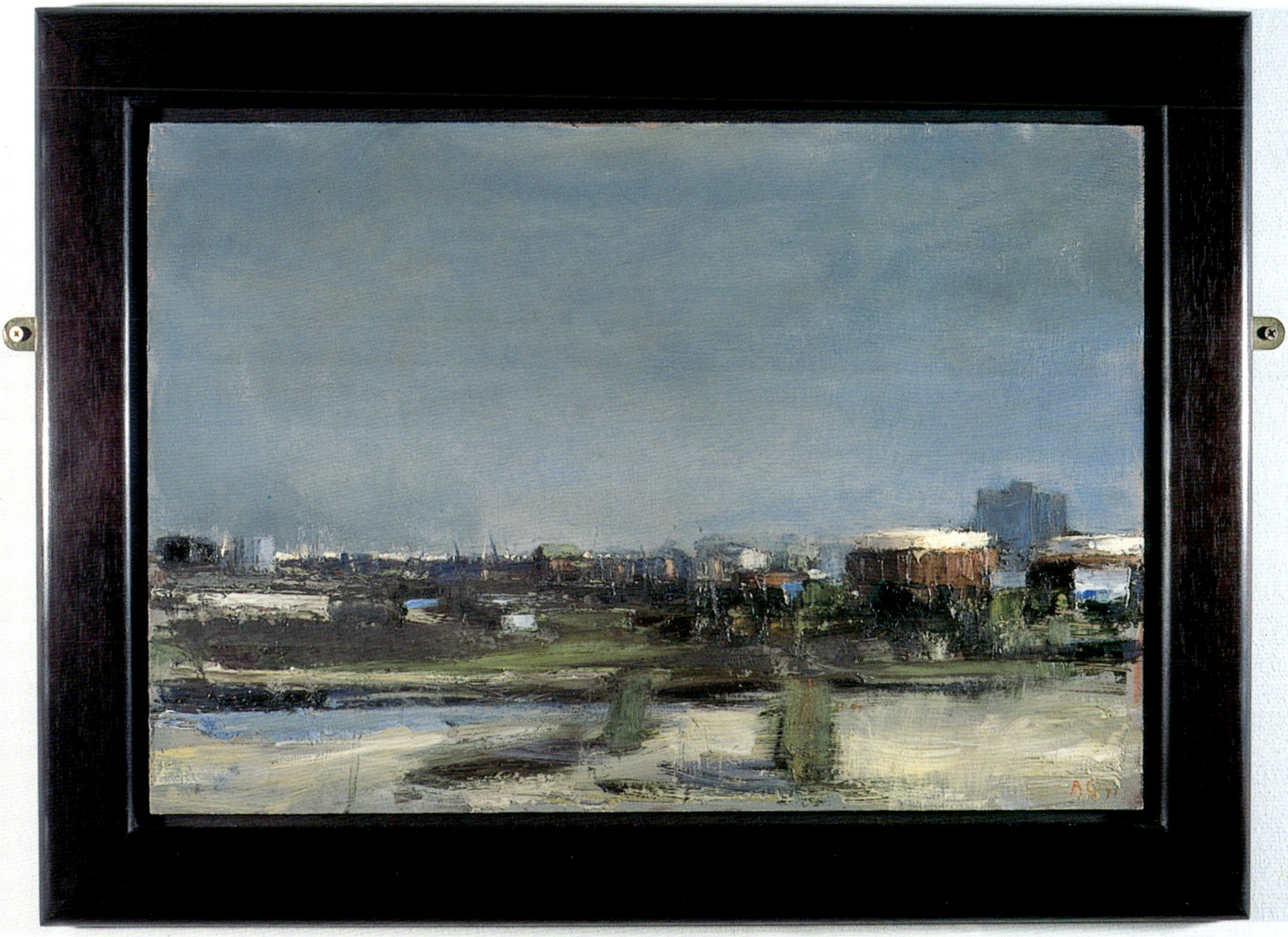

DATE 3: PETER RANDALL-PAGE MEETS EVELYN GLENNIE

Unlike many contemporary artists, sculptor Peter Randall-Page is committed to traditional materials and techniques. Since the early 1980s, Peter has gained international recognition for his immaculately cut stone sculptures. The hard, compact surface of the stone is in subtle contrast to the soft, natural forms which he likes to carve, such as shells, spirals, and the shape of fruit.

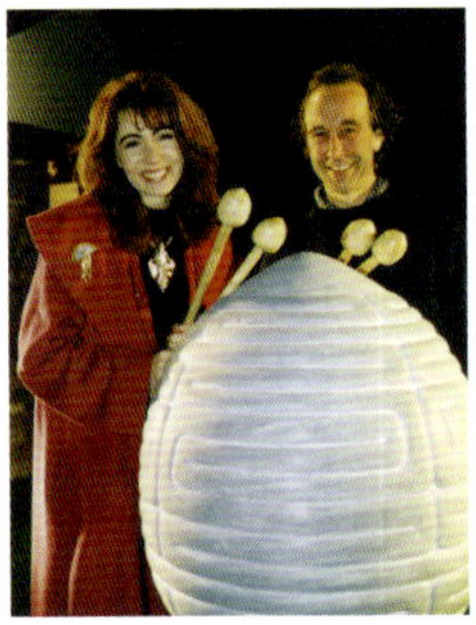

The ancient character of stone excites him: "I'm drawn to its age and beauty" he says. "The fact that it was around long before human beings means that it can confront us with a sense of our own existence in a way that something second-hand or man-made cannot." Peter also loves the directness of his craft: "One of the joys of carving is that it is such a very simple idea. You just take away the bits that you don't like, that's all there is to it."

For Peter, the carving process has striking parallels with music. The activity itself is strongly percussive. "When you are carving with someone else you inevitably fall into rhythmic patterns which evolve and flow and develop, like a kind of stone concerto. Also, when you choose a stone in a quarry, you can tell if it's a good block by hitting it. If it has a good clear ring then it isn't cracked. When I'm carving and I get a shape right, it's almost as if it kind of hums, or vibrates. I've thought for a long time about trying to make something in stone which would look very good, have a strong visual and tactile feeling, but would also move into this other area of sound and vibration – a sort of percussive sculpture."

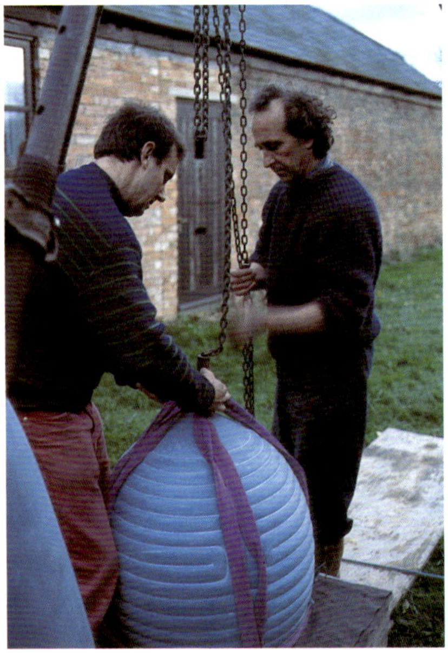

It seemed natural, therefore, that Peter should choose for his date the internationally renowned percussionist, Evelyn Glennie. Evelyn was delighted at the prospect of meeting a sculptor. "Whenever I go to a museum and see a wonderful piece of sculpture", she said, "the first thing I want to do is to touch it, or strike it. When I see a shape, very often sounds come into my mind. The sound that an instrument makes is all to do with the shape."

At their first meeting they found they had much in common. For each, the physical investment they have in their art is crucial. Evelyn, who is profoundly deaf, likes to perform barefoot in order to feel more acutely the vibrations her instrument is making. "One of the things I like about carving", said Peter, "is that you're totally involved in the physical world. It's a kind of meditation which frees you to follow your intuition about how a shape should be."

Evelyn told Peter she would like something made for her garden. "I always feel that when people are waiting at the front door there should be something interesting there to occupy them: to look at, or tap at, or be curious towards. It would be nice to have something welcoming in that space", she said.

The first stage in creating the work was for Peter to make lots of drawings, from which he decided upon a simple mushroom-like shape. He then chose an Italian marble which he thought would have a good sound to it. The stone he selected was turned on a lathe at the quarry to hollow it out, like a bell. Next, it was transported from Italy to Peter's studio where he spent ten days carving it into its finished form. The carving on the surface of the sculpture is one continuous coil. It is based on a maze design, so that if you follow the line around it comes back to the beginning.

After a laborious afternoon spent installing the work outside Evelyn's house, the unveiling finally took place after dark. Evelyn was thrilled. She was impressed that Peter had preserved the smoothness of touch and the simplicity of shape of his earlier work, whilst adding the dimension of sound.

Peter brought along some specially made mallets, so that the percussive properties of the sculpture could be tested. After Peter had given a brief demonstration, hitting and scraping the ribbed shell of the work, Evelyn took over, exploring with noisy relish its full musical range. "The village will think I've gone absolutely nuts", she said. "Its great to have something that I can smash without worrying that it will fall to pieces."

The date finished with a moonlit duet. The musician and the carver moving animatedly around the strange hybrid drum-sculpture, striking furiously at its surfaces, like high priests of some primitive musical cult.

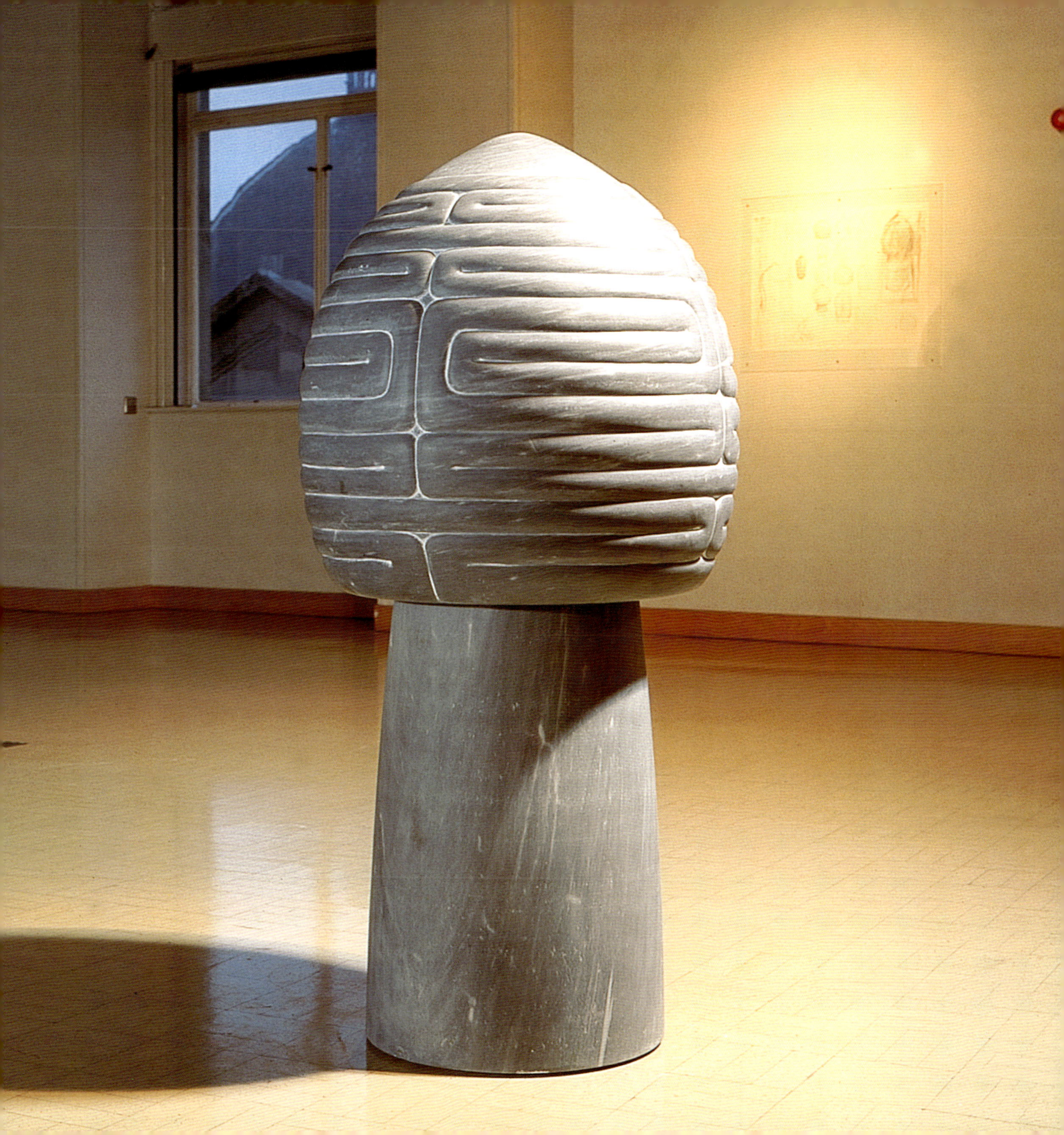

DATE 4: CATHERINE YASS MEETS CHARLES ARCHER & LILY FRENCH

Catherine Yass makes colourful light-box images of people in particular places and, sometimes, of places without people. In 1995 she was invited to make work for a 19th-century psychiatric institution, Springfield Hospital, in London. She produced a series of empty corridors which were at the same time claustrophobic and dingy, yet radiant and intense. Originally photographed as backdrops for portraits, Catherine felt that these passageways had a powerful presence in their own right. When people are included in her images they always have a strong relationship to the place where they are shown. She enters into a dialogue with her subjects to find out about their history and then works with them to construct a scene which she hopes will reflect their personality. The aim is for the person and the place to merge together in an image which reveals the character of both.

The shimmering blue effect that gives Catherine's light-boxes their distinctive character is arrived at through a very particular technique, which she discovered by accident. "I take two shots every time I photograph something, one straight after the other", she explains. "The second one I take comes out as a blue negative. I found that out by mistake when I loaded the camera wrongly once. I did lots of experiments using different films, filters, loading techniques and processes. In the end I found I preferred the blue-negative effect because the blue sort of hovers, so that you can never quite read the depth of the image. It balances all the more positive and focused, hard and fast things." Catherine's photographs, then, are made up of a positive image and a blue negative taken a second later. She likes the idea that time passing is thereby captured in the image.

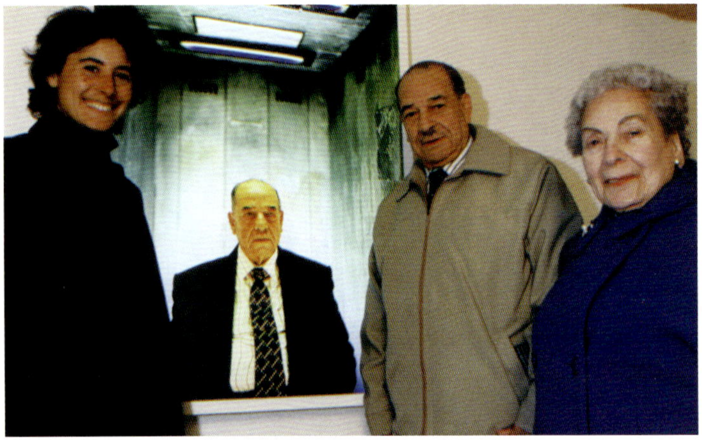

"I'm interested", says Catherine, "in photographing people whose experiences I wouldn't normally be able to imagine. I couldn't imagine, for example, what it must be like to be twice my age." A curiosity to find out led her to a date with Charles Archer and Lily French, two senior citizens on the verge of a new start in life. When Catherine met them they were about to move into a new home. "I'm interested in what it's like for them to be moving – the sense of anticipation," she said. "I'm not sure how it will come out, but I want to do something about the relationship between where they are and where they're going to."

Catherine decided to make portraits of Lily and Charles sitting in the comfort of their present homes. She also wanted to photograph their home-to-be, Grange Court, a tower block in Hackney which had fallen into disrepair and was being rebuilt as a secure residence for older people. Catherine felt that there were interesting parallels to draw between Grange Court and Charles and Lily. "I'm curious about the building being in the same state as them, of having a history and then having something new about to happen as well – being in a state of waiting." As was the case with some of Catherine's previous projects, the character of the place, Grange Court, was beginning to impose itself on her imagination: "I'm beginning to feel that I've got a date with the building as much as the people. The building is really beginning to dominate my mind."

Catherine wasn't happy that the first series of photographs she took had succeeded in capturing the feeling of personal drama she was after. "What I came up with was quite formal and didn't really say anything about what was happening", she said. Catherine only began to get a strong sense of person allied to a powerful sense of place on her way home from visiting Charles Archer. "Mr Archer told me a story about being mugged in the lift, and when I left him and went down in the lift I started to imagine how frightening that would be. It's really tiny, really smelly and very dark, an incredibly unpleasant place", she shuddered. Catherine decided to try to capture something of the intensity of Charles Archer's ordeal by making a light-box portrait of him in the lift where it had happened.

The finished work was presented to Charles and Lily in the empty flat that was to be Charles Archer's new home. The couple were astonished by how vivid and life-like the image was. "It's marvellous", enthused Lily, "though you've made him much better looking than he really is. If we ever decide to get married, would you come and take our wedding photos, dear?" she asked.

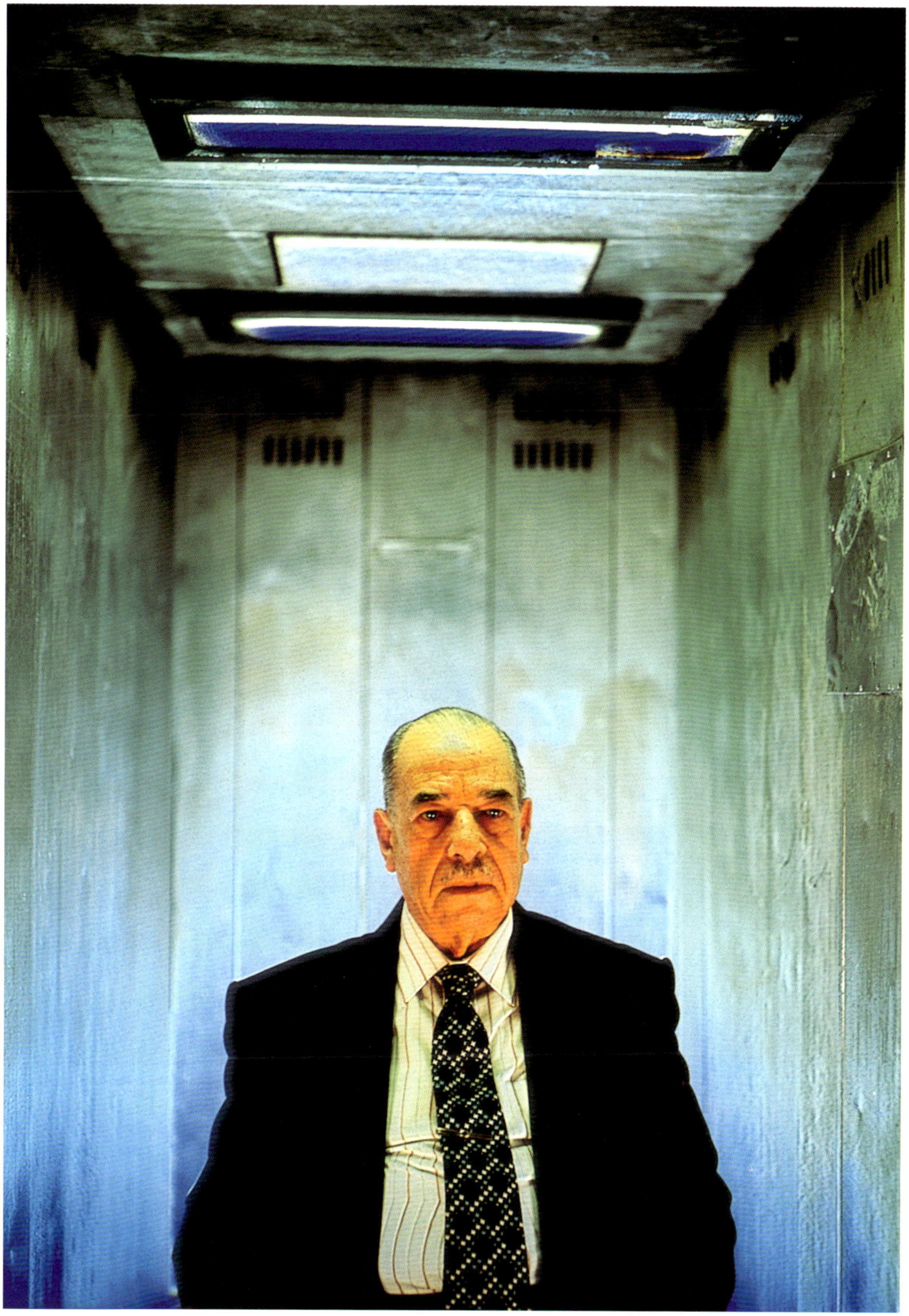

DATE 5: CHRIS OFILI MEETS ANTHONY ISMOND

Chris Ofili discovered the artistic potential of dung – its faecal attraction – on a visit to Zimbabwe in 1992. This trip to Africa, where his parents had lived before settling in Manchester, made Chris rethink his approach to painting. He decided that the things he was working on at the time: "just seemed ridiculous – the colours had nothing to do with what was going on around me, and it seemed abstract to the point of being silly. So I dried out some dung that was lying around and stuck it onto the painting." Instantly recognising that it opened up a whole new range of possibilities for his art, Chris packed some elephant dung for his flight home. Dung is now an essential ingredient of his paintings. It interrupts the decorative surface of his richly textured canvases, making sure that they never become too seductive. "I wanted to bring the beauty and decorativeness of the paintings together with the apparent ugliness of shit and make them exist in a twilight zone", he explained. Creating something gorgeous that, at the same time, "you can't really ever feel comfortable with".

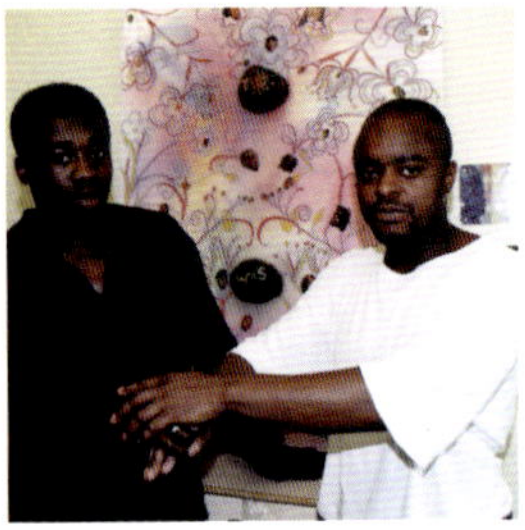

The way in which Chris likes to work is influenced by music, especially by hip-hop and jazz. His complex painting style, where many elements are brought together in unexpected combinations, is a bit like the way that hip-hop samples sounds and ideas from different sources. It was a love of hip-hop that led Chris to his date.

"I listen to hip-hop all day on the radio", says Chris, "and often the DJs will read out letters from prisoners saying, like, 'hi, don't forget me'." Struck by the idea that someone leading such a different life to himself should tune-in to the same radio shows, Chris decided he'd like to make contact with a hip-hop loving inmate. He felt confident that, though their experiences would be different in so many respects, they would find a bond through their shared passion for the music. Chris was not interested to pass judgement on what his date had done, "I just want to connect with him as a person", he said.

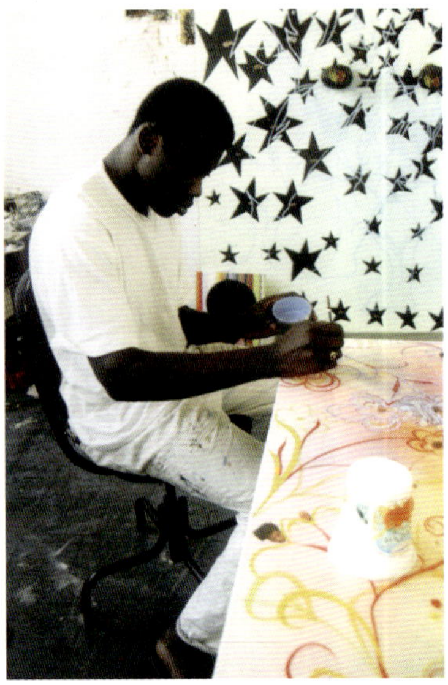

Anthony Ismond, who was gearing up for a second year at Wormwood Scrubs, welcomed the chance to meet someone who could make something to brighten up the bleak cell that would be his home until the year 2000. "The things I like to look at", he told Chris, "are things to do with hip-hop culture". The drabness of Anthony's cell walls was interrupted by the occasional hip-hop related photograph cut from music magazines: stars of rap, like Lil' Kim and Snoop Doggy Dog.

Chris felt quite overwhelmed by his trip to the Scrubs. "I'd just have been happy to have met Anthony, to have experienced the prison and that would be it", he said. "But now I've got to deal with making something. God, what am I gonna do?" He decided in the end that he wanted to make something very personal to Anthony, nothing too deep and conceptual, nothing to do with the shock of visiting the jail. Chris felt it best to make something beautiful to soften the gloom of the environment. As he anticipated, music was to be an important key to connecting .

Chris made one of his trademark paintings, a bright and busy composite of paint, dung, varnish, glitter and photos. The photographs were of mutual hip-hop idols, like Foxy Brown and the Notorious B.I.G. As a special touch, Chris inscribed Anthony's nickname, TISWAS, onto the surface of the solidified dung with coloured map pins. The result was richly decorative. "The word decorative", said Chris, "is often used in the art world in a negative sense, but to me it's one of the greatest compliments that somebody could pay my work. I've decided to make things that are really beautiful to look at in a world where everyone else seems to be trying to sell ideas."

"Nice one!" was Anthony's immediate reaction when Chris carried the work into his cell. He was a bit taken aback to learn that the two large brown lumps bearing his nickname were made up of 100 per cent real elephant dung from London Zoo, but, when it became clear that the pong had been neutralised, he soon warmed to the idea. "Now that's what you call art, innit", he beamed.

Unfortunately, though, the prison environment threatened to be too brutal to house Chris's delicate painting. "It's the sort of place", says Chris, "where nice things easily get spoiled and where the guys don't want to have possessions that are gonna draw attention to them." The painting is now back in Chris's custody, where it will remain until Anthony finishes his stretch.

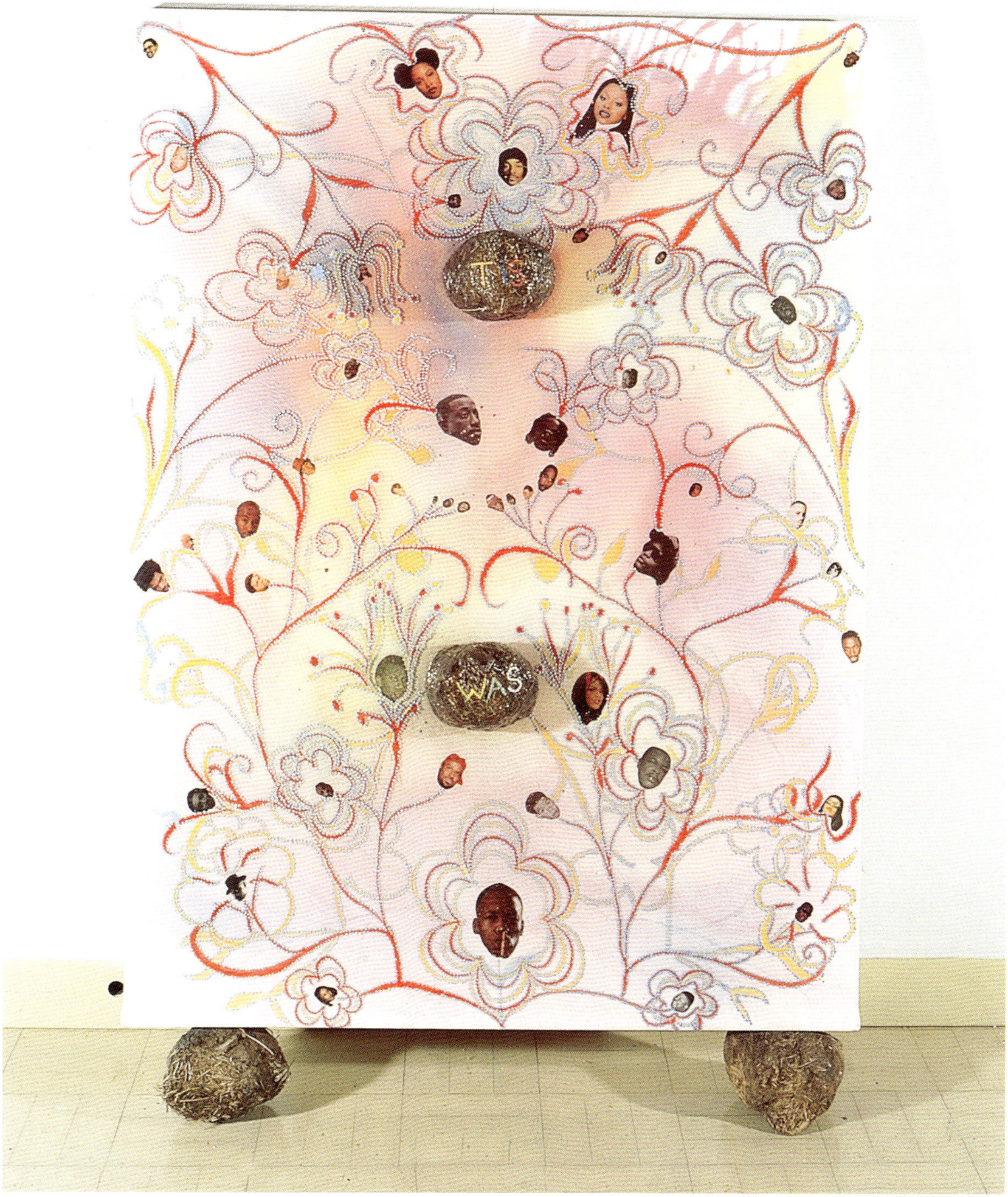
WAS

DATE 6: BRAD LOCHORE MEETS ANYA HURLBERT

Painting is often thought of as a window opening onto an imaginary world. The world of Brad Lochore's paintings is a world without substance, a silent world of shadows and illusions. "At the end of the 20th century", says Brad, "we are confronted by a constant stream of images. I see my shadow paintings as pauses in that stream." His shadows, shown in perspective, give the impression of having been genuinely observed. They are, however, entirely made up. "All my paintings", explains Brad, "are to a large degree a process of seduction and betrayal. You are drawn into an image and at the same time betrayed by it; for example, by a perspective that fails to lead anywhere. What I am interested in is confusing the eye: saying one thing and meaning another."

Brad was very keen to meet up with Anya Hurlbert, a vision scientist at Newcastle University. "Anya", said Brad, "has been doing a similar sort of investigation to me, but from an entirely different angle; the scientific angle. I hope she'll be able to teach me something that I can adapt to my way of painting."

Anya was also intrigued by what she could learn from the date: "Artists make images in order to set off experiences in the viewer's mind, and I look at images to try and understand what sort of mental processes they might trigger. My work involves making images which are very much simpler than what an artist makes, and not nearly as beautiful. I'm very keen to sit Brad down in front of some of our visual stimuli and see how he reacts; see whether as an artist he has a different sort of visual brain to the normal observer."

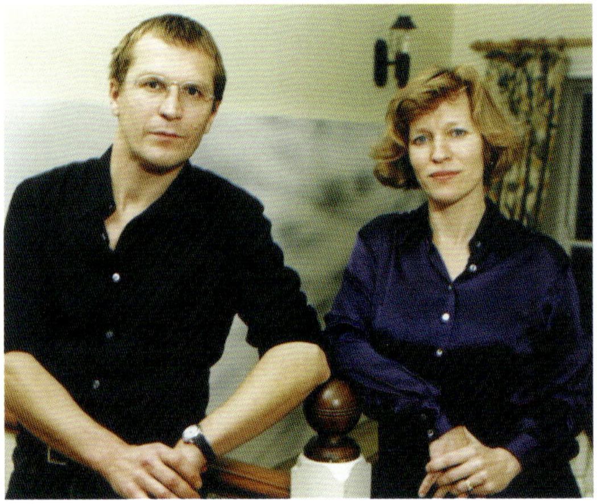

At their first meeting, in the painter's studio, Anya was deeply impressed by Brad's ability to conjure up beautiful illusions. "They're the most real shadows I've ever seen," she said . "It's very disorienting to walk in and see shadows of objects that aren't there. I feel like I'm in a room full of non-existent objects. It's fabulous."

"Anya kept apologising", said Brad, "for the fact that she found the work beautiful, but to a large degree that's exactly what the work's about. Beauty draws the viewer in; it makes you feel your desires are fulfilled."

Back in her Newcastle laboratory Anya concocted a shadow illusion of her own for Brad to decipher, which he did with aplomb. "I'm deeply impressed by the way you were able to unpick it", she told him. "The shadow is enabling us to see what we could not actually see in real life. I would love to see you paint an impossible shadow, particularly a coloured shadow. It would teach me about what makes coloured shadows look real." It was a challenge that Brad couldn't resist.

On the way back from his trip Brad was struck by an impression of light flashing through the trees that lined the route. It gave him the idea of creating, back in his studio, a shadow cast by foliage upon a wall. Brad simulated the effect of glimpsing shadows through a car window by using real plants and artificial lighting. He drew onto canvas a kind of stencil, mapping where the different coloured shadows had fallen, and then proceeded to paint them in, a painstaking process which took many hours of studious concentration. The task of mixing the subtle shades, alone, took half a day.

After visiting Anya's home, Brad had decided to make a painting for her stairwell. "Moving up and down stairs will give a lot of different possible angles on it", he noted. "People expect a perfect point of view when they come to see a work in the gallery, but most of life's not like that."

When the finished work was unveiled to Anya she recognised immediately the dynamism that Brad had tried to capture. "There's an incredible amount of movement in it", she observed. "It's got what we scientists call 'motion blur'." Anya was deeply absorbed by the complexity of the painting. For all its deceptive simplicity, it was filled with nuances of light and motion which multiplied with every change of light or viewpoint. Each attempt to unravel its enigmas threw up new possibilities of interpretation. "In the end", said Anya, "it defies analysis."

The date had confirmed Brad's perception of the fundamental difference between their activities. "For Anya", noted Brad, "science is a way of discovering things which makes the world more coherent, but my project is, essentially, against coherence."

DATE 7: NINA SAUNDERS MEETS SALLY LESLIE

Nina Saunders left her native Denmark to come to England at the age of seventeen. She developed a distinctive sculptural style based around discarded furniture, particularly chairs, whilst studying at London's Central St Martin's College of Art & Design. Nina's works tread a fine line between opposites: between beauty and repulsion, humour and dread, and homeliness and alienation. Swollen forms recur in many of her chairs; oversized and grotesque, like tumorous growths. This swelling first emerged in *Are You Sitting Comfortably*, 1990. In this sculpture any sense of the comfiness of the chair is undermined by the bulbous lump that has replaced one of its arms and most of its seat. Her work inhabits the realm of the uncanny, where feelings of both amusement and unease are evoked by the ordinary made strange.

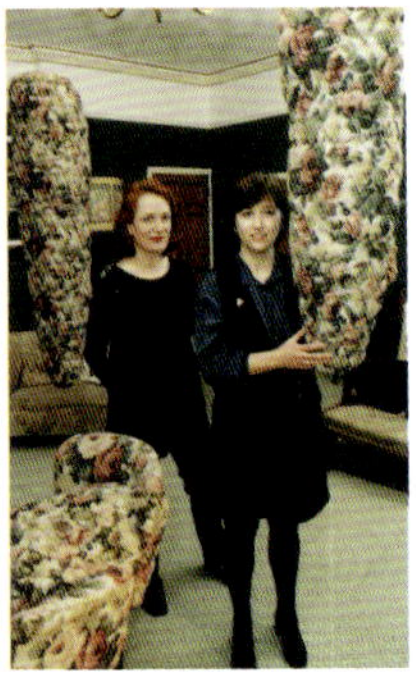

"Why chairs?", asks Nina, "it's because of the way that we so easily identify with chairs, they're very familiar things to us because they accommodate our bodies. Chairs are very adaptable and have a great deal of personality; they all have a story to tell." It was the personality of one particular chair that led Nina to her date, the beekeeper Sally Leslie.

"When I found it on a street corner it was a pretty disgusting chair, with springs coming out of it", she recalled. "It's a very old-fashioned chair with a beautiful pattern and a sort of female form and when I saw it I knew immediately that it had to do with bee-keeping, but I didn't know why. That was the starting point for that chair, which has been with me now for about a year." Nina also felt a strong desire to visit Dorset. "Why Dorset? It always felt like the most exciting place to me because of all the bumps and hills and the sea. Although very different from my homeland, it felt like going home."

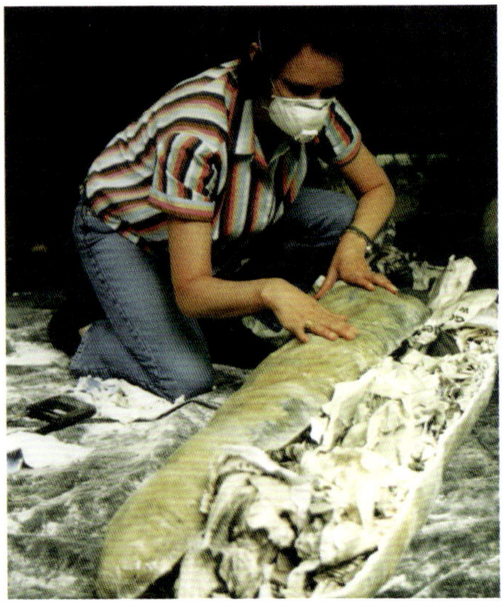

Amateur beekeeper Sally Leslie was intrigued by the prospect of an artist making work for her house on the Isle of Portland. Sally regrets that: "at school art appreciation classes just passed me by. I was bored to tears. Now I love it, though I don't really understand modern art. I work in a quarry where sculptors and carvers frequently come. The carvers can just look at a block of stone and imagine how they can make something from it. That fascinates me."

If Sally didn't know much about modern art, Nina, in her turn, confessed: "I don't know a hell of a lot about bees." After meeting Sally and her bees, however, and soaking up the home environment, Nina got very excited about the notion of swarming and felt that that should become the focus of her work. "I asked Sally in her wonderful sitting room where would the bees go if they came into the room, maybe around the chandelier or under the table?" The idea for the work then started to embrace not only the chair but the whole room as well.

Although Nina never actually saw the bees swarm, she got an idea of how it would look from a photograph on Sally's living-room wall. "I was very struck by the collective energy as well as by the beautiful sculptural form that the bees made", she said. Nina returned to her studio to begin working towards an ambitious installation that would take her six months of hard work to complete. As well as adapting the original chair so that it appeared to be bursting its seams with a bulging swarming mass, Nina made three vast pendulous upholstered forms to hang from Sally's ceiling, like chandeliers enveloped by bees. In order to suggest something of the texture of the swarming, she studded the surfaces with 1500 tiny bee-shaped buttons. Anxious to ensure that her bold intervention wouldn't disturb too much the harmony of Sally's room, Nina made sure that her date was consulted on the choice of fabric.

Upon entering her impressively transformed sitting-room for the first time, Sally was amazed by the accuracy with which Nina had managed to capture the swarming effect. "It's exactly the shape the bees would make", she confirmed. As well as admiring the strong visual and sculptural presence of her upholstered art work, Sally was absorbed by its luxurious tactile quality. "It's absolutely gorgeous, I just want to hug it", she drooled.

Nina was flattered by her date's enthusiastic response but, sadly, the critics she would really have liked to impress were unable to attend the Private View. "When I was making it", revealed the perfection-seeking sculptress, "I was constantly wondering 'but would the bees be pleased'?"

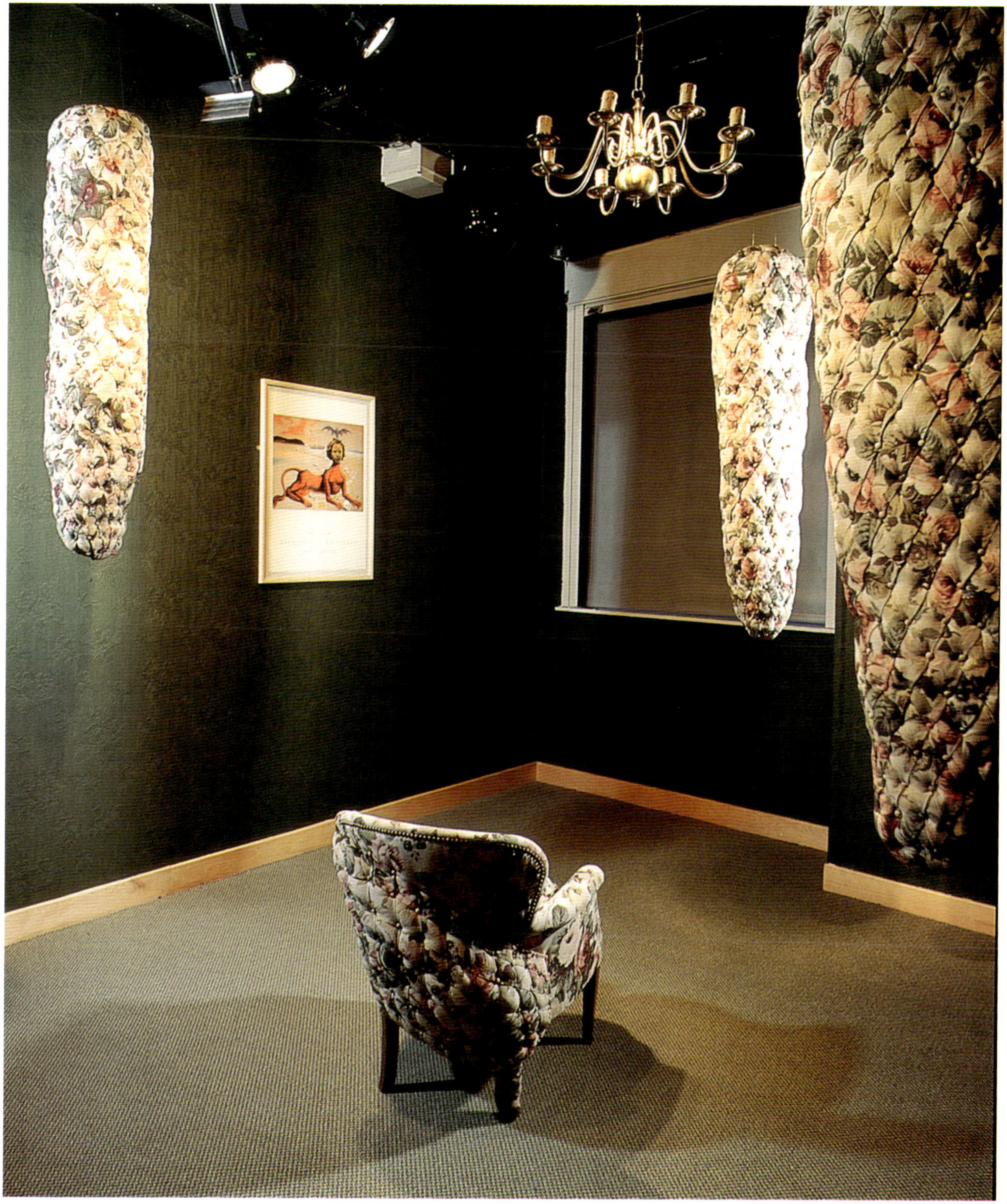

DATE 8: HADRIAN PIGOTT MEETS JOHN BUTCHER

"The work I've made to date has been very much to do with the domestic environment", says Hadrian Pigott, "and to do with the flip side of objects – the way that they're not supposed to work really." Hadrian's 1994 work, Instrument of Hygiene, consists of an old-fashioned wash basin with soaps and copper fittings housed in a leather case lined with red velvet, like a surreal version of a deluxe briefcase, or a travelling case for musical instruments. One of several works that Hadrian has made involving soap, it seems to imply that its owner has a washing disorder; that we are all, perhaps, obsessed with cleanliness. Instrument of Hygiene plays on both the sculptural characteristics of household items and on the meanings and feelings they evoke. A common feature of Hadrian's work is the unravelling of form from function: taking something real and useful and ending up with something refined, but purely abstract and useless.

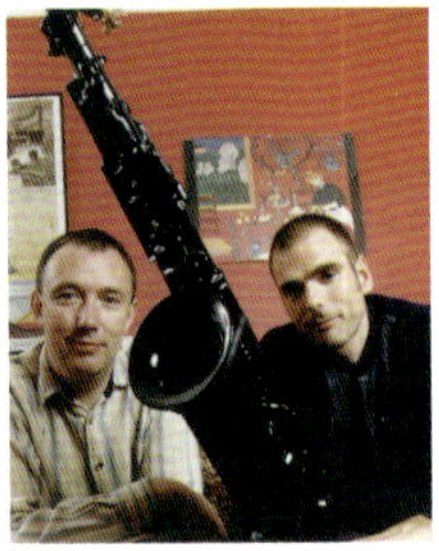

Recognising his own compulsive attraction to certain kinds of objects, Hadrian wanted a date with "somebody who had a very definite relationship with an object, to an extreme degree". Whilst pondering who this might be, he came across musician John Butcher at a gig in a south London pub. "When John started playing I realised that he was doing something absolutely extraordinary with the saxophone", recalls Hadrian. "I decided that to try to understand what he's doing with that item, and to try to make something from that would be very interesting."

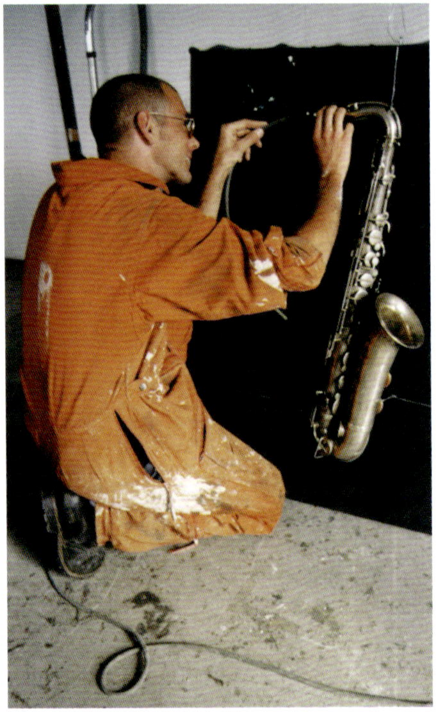

John Butcher recognises that dedication to his music has led him to neglect other kinds of art. He therefore regarded a date with Hadrian as "a chance to restimulate myself". Although sharing Hadrian's interest in exploring artistic boundaries, John feels that, in general, musicians and visual artists have a very different approach to creativity: "Visual artists work alone. I do my creative work with other musicians in front of a live audience." Hadrian tends to agree: "Free-form jazz is a very long way from the careful, calculated work that I do. Also, sculpture deals with real objects, whereas music is invisible and transient."

John told Hadrian that he would like a work made for his practice-room at home. The time spent here represents: "the time when I'd be most interested in paying attention to some piece of visual art, not in another room more associated with day-to-day living." Hadrian was very receptive to this idea: "John's music lives in that small room and that's really what I want to make a piece of work about."

Hadrian decided "to make a version of the saxophone that is recognisable in the same way that the music John plays is recognisable, but somehow indistinct as well. It will imply trying and almost getting something, striving to reach something. I want to base it on a full- sized saxophone. Something that John can get his hands on, something tangible".

The search for an instrument around which to make the work led Hadrian to a pawnbroker's shop in Islington. Having found a suitable sax, the next stage was to carry out experiments in rubber casting. The aim was to lose the shape of the saxophone and yet somehow to retain it. Latex was chosen as the best material from which to make a mould for the sculpture because: "latex is a fantastic stretching material which allows you to preserve quite a lot of information about what's in it but also obscures quite a lot." The final object was to be made of painted fibreglass. Following much trial and error and a number of faults in the casting process, Hadrian finally arrived at a shape and texture he was happy with. After several days of painstaking sanding, polishing and painting, the immaculate jet-black sculpture was ready for delivery.

At the unveiling ceremony, John was surprised to see that Hadrian had opted to work so literally with the form of his instrument. Hadrian explained that it had been important to create something that looked as though it could be played, something so seductive that you would really want to know what it would sound like. In making the work he had tried to imagine what it was like to reach for something that would forever be just out of range. As the title he gave the work, Mute, implies, though, this is one instrument whose musical secret John Butcher will never uncover.

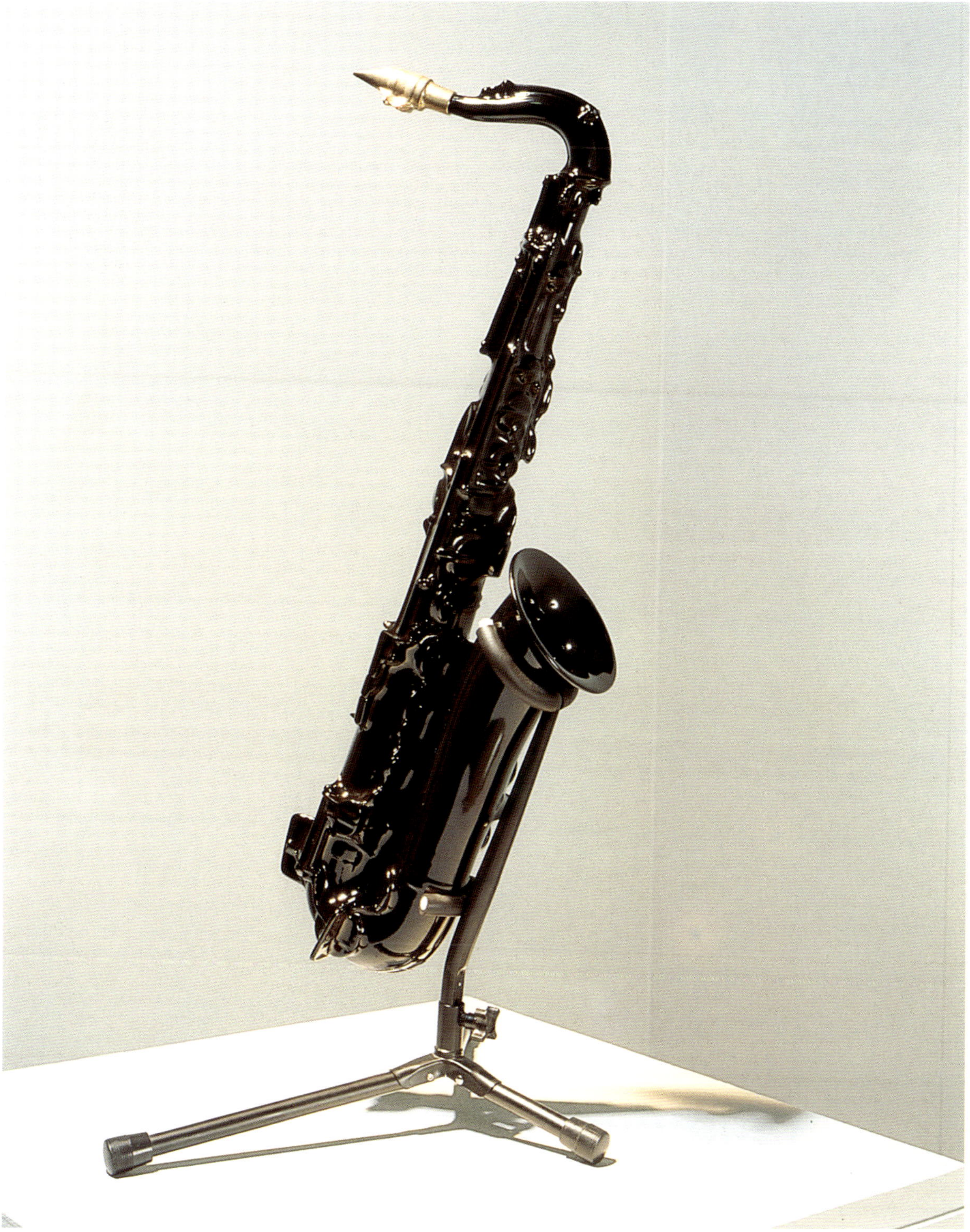

DATE 9: JAKE & DINOS CHAPMAN MEET JUSTINE FRISCHMANN

Jake and Dinos Chapman have been called "the Burke and Hare of Contemporary British art". "These boys", said one critic, "make Damien Hirst look like the Angel Gabriel." Having started off as individual artists, they chose to team up because: "We're only good enough to make one person's work; our own work is crap." The brothers launched their 'terrorist aesthetic' on the world, in 1992, with their first joint exhibition We Are Artists. Since then, they have unleashed a steady barrage of provocative, deliberately shocking art works and manifestos, one of which declared: "I want to rub salt into your inferiority complex, smash your ego in the face, gouge your eyes from their sockets and piss in the empty holes." Like versions of Dr Frankenstein for the 1990s, their works resemble a perverted assembly-line of toy-store body parts. Although intended to outrage, not to moralise, these freak-show sculptures have been seen by some as a comment on the perils of unregulated science. "Genetic engineering claims to move towards some idea of purity", says Jake, "our work spoils that idea."

In deciding upon a suitable date, the Chapman brothers sensibly recognised that their work wouldn't be to everyone's taste. They wanted to feel confident that they'd be choosing someone who wouldn't be turned off by their provocative art. "After all", said Jake, "you wouldn't tell a sick joke at a dinner party where you didn't know the guests". They opted for Justine Frischmann from the pop band Elastica, hoping that someone accustomed to a 'sex, drugs and rock'n'roll' lifestyle might find their off-beat creations quite appealing.

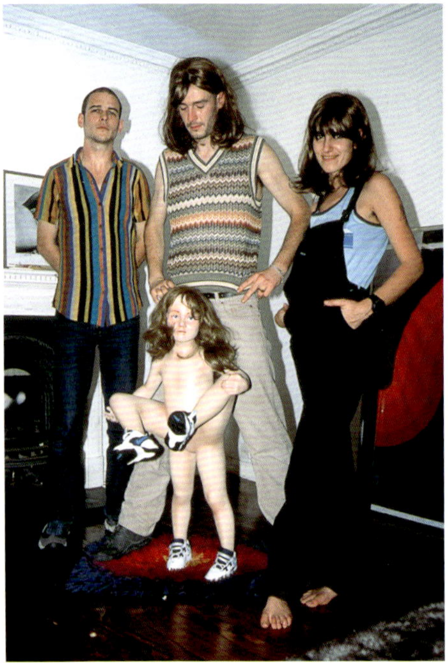

Justine was already vaguely familiar with Jake and Dinos's work, but didn't want to find out too much before she'd had a chance to see it at first hand. "I'd like to react to it on my own terms, without knowing what the official line is", she said. Justine decided that she'd like the brothers to make something to liven up her bedroom. "Bear in mind", she warned, "that it's the first thing I'll see in the morning and the last thing I'll see at night, so I'll probably end up dreaming about it."

Not overly concerned about the prospect of giving their date nightmares, Jake and Dinos initially thought of making a gruesome wall panel: a bank of earth dotted with skulls, with blood red liquid pouring from their eyes and mouths into a trough full of exotic flowers. Justine was not hugely taken with the idea. "I'd prefer something that reminds me of sex, rather than death, in my bedroom", she said. Justine was much more enamoured by the multi-genitalled mannequin works which the brothers showed her during a visit to their studio. Her mind was made up. "They're really beautiful and incredibly sexy and I'd absolutely love one of those", she declared.
Surprisingly perhaps, considering their reputation, the 'bad boys' of British art were only too happy to oblige. Unlike some contemporary artists who rely on the skills of others to make things for them, Jake and Dinos put a lot of time and effort into their immaculately crafted works. Each tiny hand-painted freckle on the faces of their carefully malformed creatures has been lovingly applied. The final effect is so seamless, points out Dinos, that once finished the mutant mannequins "don't even look like they've been made". The discrepancy between the glossy perfection of the craftsmanship and the shocking abnormality of the end product contributes to the disturbing impact of their work.

In recognition, perhaps, of its prominently positioned male member and the fact that it had a couple more limbs than is considered usual, the Chapman brothers called their creation *Cockroach Kid*. Justine was thrilled to have such a compelling presence in her bedroom, but wasn't afraid to make suggestions about how it might be improved. "Can I have it without the wig?", she asked. Pop-world friends attending the Private View were also anxious that the full potential of the sculpture should be explored. It was suggested that the creature might perhaps look better on all fours, or should that be all sixes?

Not wishing to be overly protective towards their latest off-spring, Jake and Dinos agreed that whatever Justine chose to do with the *Cockroach Kid* in the privacy of her own bedroom was entirely up to her. "When I'm left to my own devices I'm definitely going to be dressing it up and messing about with it", she promised. "It's a good thing that it's out of the gallery environment and I can interfere with it."

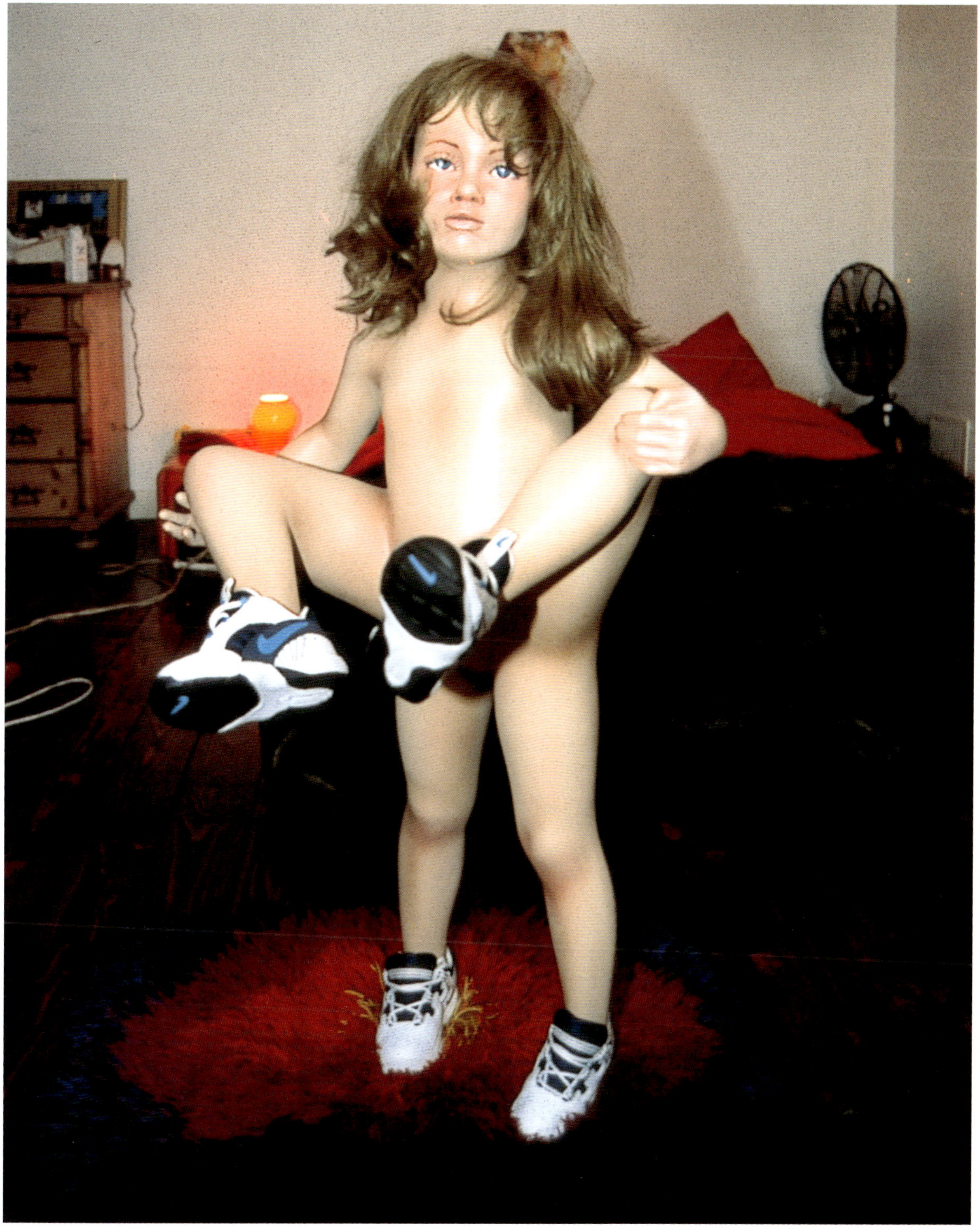

DATE 10: SAM TAYLOR WOOD MEETS ALASTAIR MORRISON

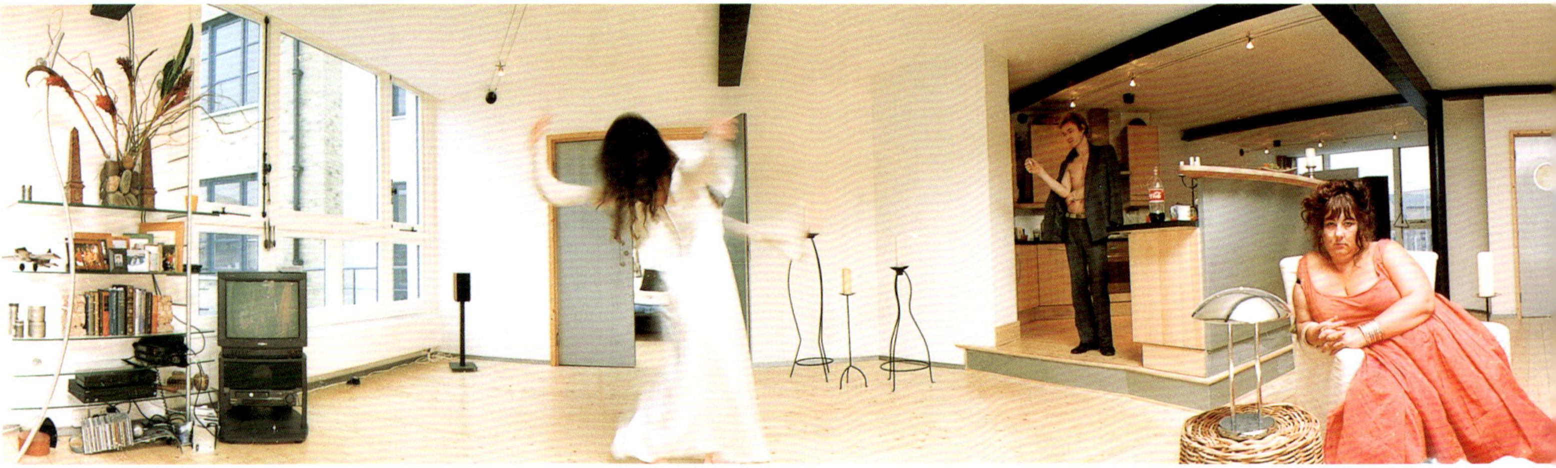

Since graduating from Goldsmith's College, London, in 1990, Sam Taylor-Wood has gain recognition as one of the leading Young British Artists (YBAs) who are currently causing a stir on the art scene in the UK and abroad. Sam uses photography, film, video installation and sound, often combining two or more of these to create works which play with notions of identity and explore unspoken tensions in the relationships between the subjects whom she records. In one recent work, made for the TV series Expanding Pictures, Sam filmed the actress and pop star Kylie Minogue miming to a recording of the last castrato singing. Kylie was filmed topless, from the back, which added to the gender confusion: a beautiful young woman with a boyish body mouthing the words of a man who had had surgery to make him sound like a woman.

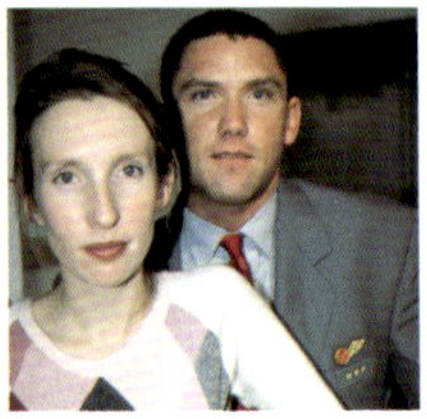

Such works have an enigmatic quality, and it is Sam's interest in creating mysterious dramas that has recently led her to create a series of photographic works entitled Five Revolutionary Seconds. These images involve a special 360-degree camera which takes a picture of an entire room and its inhabitants, who are often captured in intimate and vulnerable situations or trapped in some private emotional moment. The characters act out strange narrative-less dramas: in one a naked man leans against a doorway, while a couple argue, two people sit bored on a sofa and a man plays a piano; in another, set in a stately home, an elegant woman stands in evening dress, while two people languish on sofas and a naked couple have sex without looking at each other.

Sam explains that in interpreting these works, the viewer is "trying to find out what the relationship is between the people or why they're in these different states. It doesn't really lead you to anywhere in particular, but it moves you along the photograph. So, in a sense, you're almost reading it a bit like you would read a film."

The challenge of venturing into unknown territory appealed to Sam: "I like the idea of it being very spontaneous, seeing a place I haven't seen before, and meeting a person I haven't met before." She wanted to meet someone who would like to participate in one of her panoramic dramas, and who lived in a space large enough to stage one.

Alastair Morrison, a chief steward with a major airline, was well-used to role playing in his professional life. Being an air steward, said Alastair, is like acting; "passengers sit and watch us. It's like a show – they come along and expect happy bubbly people and, regardless of how you feel, when you put the uniform on, the show has to go on." He was only too happy to open up his spacious loft-style apartment to accommodate the project, but he hoped that Sam's photograph, despite its theatrical nature, would reflect

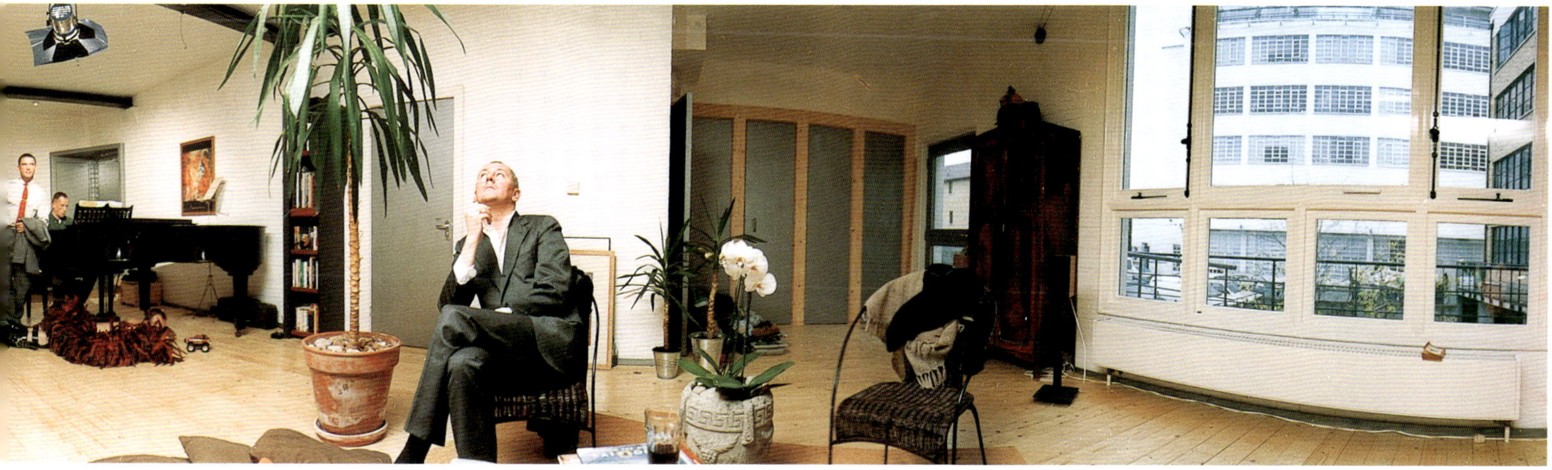

something of his real personality: "It's important for me that I am portrayed as who I am, or as one of the facets of myself."

Sam was keen for Alastair to wear his uniform for the set; initially he wasn't sure, saying, "It's just not me in this environment", but when he realised it was integral to Sam's conception of the work, he agreed to pose in it leaning against the piano that his flatmate, Michael, was playing. The cast of the scene was completed by five of Sam's friends, including one extrovert character, John, who emerged from Alastair's bathroom in a feathers and leather outfit.

Sam decided to photograph two different set-ups and arranged the models for each around the the room, with a friend, Sue, dressed in red, placed centre stage. When she saw the contact sheet, she knew instantly which she preferred: "When I make photographs I don't set out for there to be any kind of narrative that you can link together, but I do like it when things present themselves. This one looks like Sue is disgruntled with all her courtiers placed around her."

Sam hung the photograph on the wall behind Alastair's piano. What would Alastair make of his character in the mini-drama? He was impressed with the photograph, but he still had one reservation: "I'm really happy with how it turned out, but I still find it odd that I'm in my uniform." Sam herself was delighted with the outcome: "It's the first time I've used the patron inside the photograph and I think it worked well."

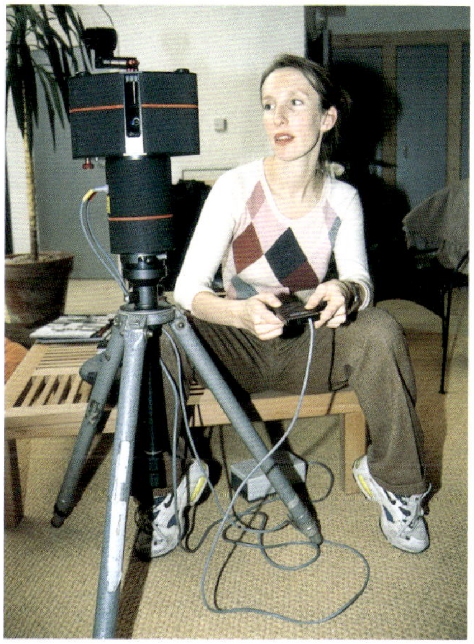

DATE 11: JULIE ROBERTS MEETS COLIN BEGG, BARRIE McKILLOP & IEN SOUN LY

Julie Roberts is best known for her eerily cool paintings of medical objects. Dentists' chairs, straitjackets and gynaecological instruments are rendered in minute detail against flat, richly coloured backgrounds. The discrepancy between Julie's smooth, seductive painting style and the sinister objects she depicts creates an uneasy tension.

Although people rarely appear directly in her works, there is often a suggestion of physical or emotional pain. Her choice of subject-matter reflects an awareness of the power that institutions – such as science, religion and even the family – hold over our lives. Julie is particularly concerned with the unequal, often damaging, treatment that women have endured at the hands of male-dominated institutions. "I tend, however, not to make judgements. My interest is in observing, and making inconclusive studies", she says.

Julie opted for a date with a household of junior doctors because of their professional connection with her area of enquiry. She was aware that the date implied an element of role-reversal. "Making paintings for three male doctors seems quite ironic considering the work that I've been doing", she said. "In a way, it will be like a stranger walking into their life to examine them. I hope they might get a sense that in this instance they're like the patient and I'm the doctor."

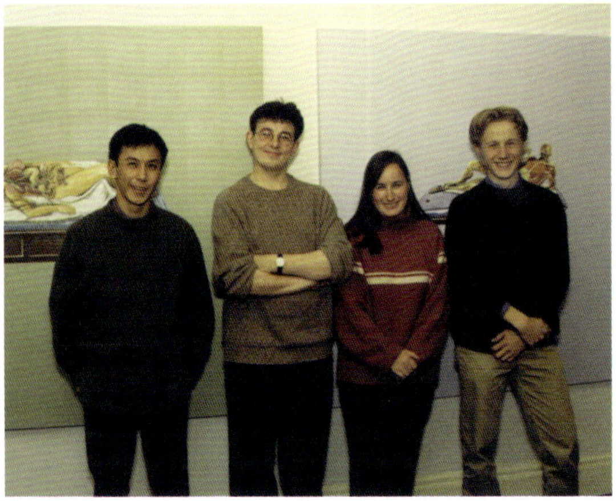

Colin, Barrie and Ien, the house-sharing doctors who agreed to be Julie's dates, have recently taken up their first appointments at various Glasgow hospitals. The science-trained trio were intrigued to meet a real-life painter. Barrie confessed to feeling "a bit short-changed at times" by the efforts of contemporary artists. Colin hoped that their date would provide food for thought: "I'm not happy just with pretty pictures. I like something that makes me think a bit more. Contemporary artists have a responsibility to try and challenge the public into new ways of looking."

Julie took her consorts to some of the sites that had influenced her previous work: to the Pathology Museum at Edinburgh's Royal College of Surgeons, and to Glasgow City Police Mortuary, which inspired some shrouded corpse paintings just after the death of her grandmother. The doctors were impressed to hear that all her paintings are meticulously researched. They were struck by how different Julie's professional interest is from their own. "Julie would come to the mortuary to get involved with the emotional side of medicine, which is totally different to why we'd be here", said Ien.

Julie decided that the time was ripe to draw upon some data she had collected from a museum in Florence, on anatomical models. They had been used by 18th-century Italian medical students to study the internal organs. "They're beautiful but macabre, very compelling", she said. "The guys will all have trained with anatomical bodies, so it should be of interest to them."

The female models, called 'Anatomical Venuses', are strikingly different from their male counterparts. Often adorned with pearl necklaces, long hair and eyelashes, they lie on silk cushions in passive, sexually alluring poses. As with some of her previous work, Julie was struck by the contrasting messages that these medical specimens gave out about gender: "the male model is usually in a kind of intellectual pose, like Michelangelo's Adam, whereas the female model is sprawled on her back with her stomach hanging out."

Julie gave the subject her customary treatment, rendering the reclining wax models in sumptuous detail, against a monochrome background: one large painting of a semi-skinned female model and another of her flayed male companion. Intended to be viewed as a pair, she titled them *Anatomical Marriage*. How, then, would the young doctors respond to this gruesome twosome?

They immediately cast a clinical eye over the gory details. "That looks like the two ends of the transverse colon", pointed out Ien, "or maybe it's the small bowel?" Moving from the particular to the general, Colin found the Venus disconcerting: "The expression on her face freaks me out. I'm not used to seeing cadavers with their eyes open." The consensus was that the doctors could live with the paintings on the communal wall, but wouldn't care to have them in their bedrooms.

Overall, the date was a great success. "We're very impressed with the work we've seen", said Barrie. "It looks nice, but then when you speak to Julie you realise that there's an awful lot more behind it as well." For her part, Julie had some of her fears about the medical profession allayed. "I expected it to be like going to the doctors", she confessed, "but it wasn't. They were really lovely."

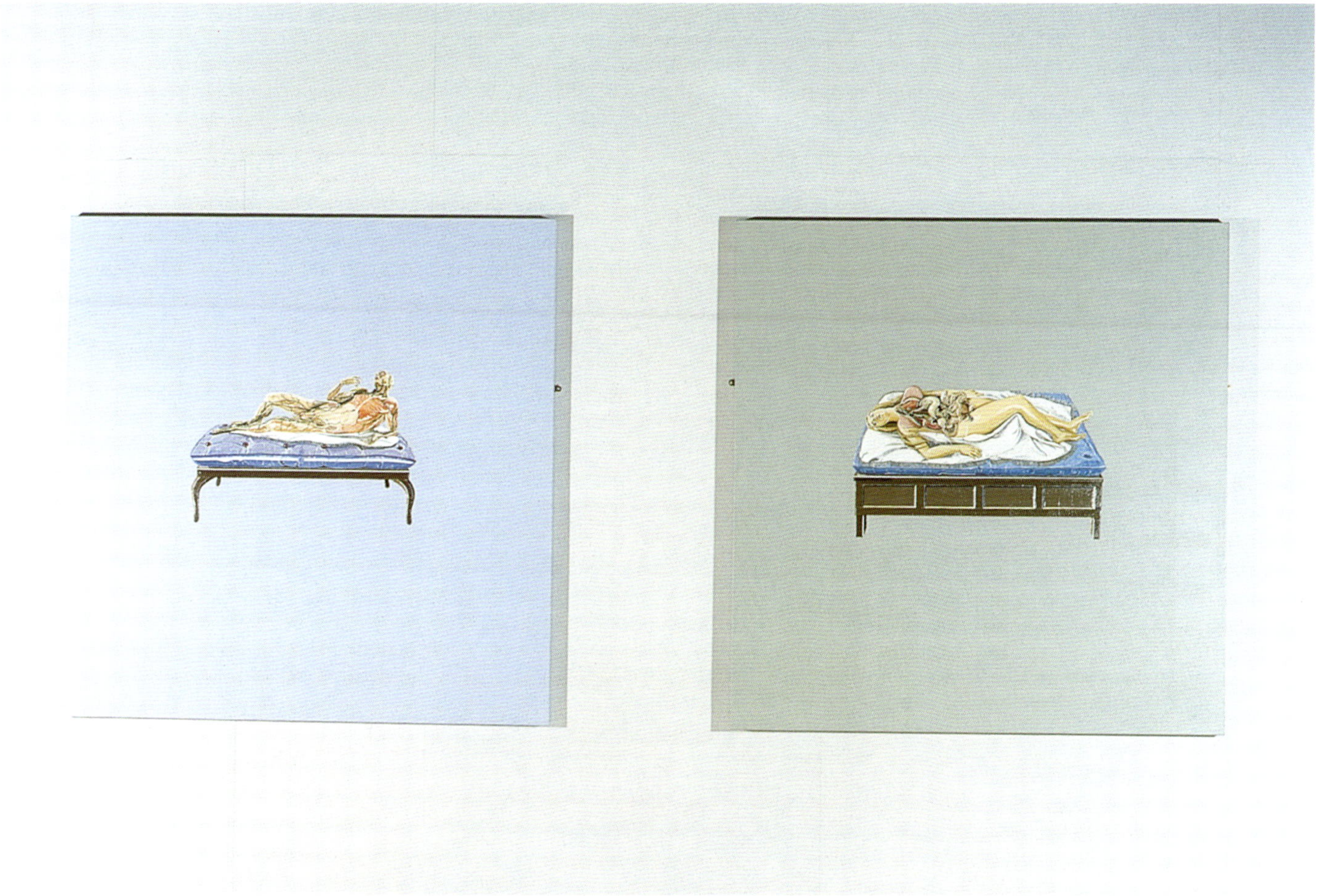

DATE 12: JESSICA VOORSANGER MEETS GARY COOK

New Yorker Jessica Voorsanger's art is about celebrity and what it's like to be 'star-struck'. The desire and the pain of fandom, the thrill and absurdity of adoration from a distance, provides the emotional raw material for her work. Like an earlier star-struck New York artist, Andy Warhol, Jessica often blurs the boundaries between art and life. Last year, the naming of her new-born baby became the subject of an exhibition, *The Baby Shower*, at London's Camden Art Gallery. The celebrities who gave their permission for Jessica's daughter to be named after them will, no doubt, be pleased to know that both mother and little miss Etta Ruby Rula Honor Twiggy Joanna Hayley Emma Jethro Voorsanger-Brill are doing just fine.

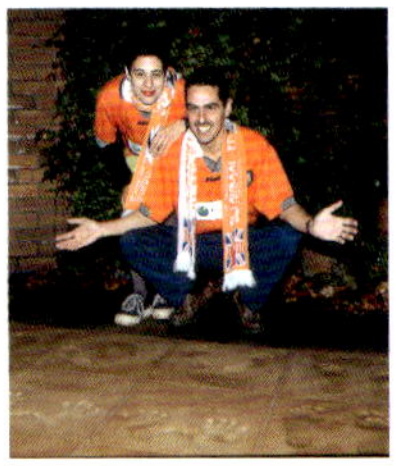

Although Jessica's art is generally humorous, she has first-hand experience of the irrational cravings of the seriously obsessed. Her own not-so-secret passion is David Cassidy. Jessica's graduation show at Goldsmith's College, London, was built around a seven-foot cut-out of the 70s pop idol. As a conceptual artist, Jessica isn't limited to just one method or technique. "I use lots of different kinds of media: mail-art, video, photography, sculpture, painting. Whatever's most appropriate to the specific idea", she says.

Jessica saw her date as a chance to meet an example of that notorious brand of irrational obsessive: the football supporter. Perhaps the most die-hard of all football fans are those who follow less glamorous teams through thick and, usually, thin. A fan of unfashionable Blackpool, resort of faded stars, was therefore decided upon. "I want to be able to visit their house", said Jessica, "and see evidence of the fact that they really love this team. Anyone who fits the criterion of absolute adoration and love for Blackpool FC is quite good enough for me."

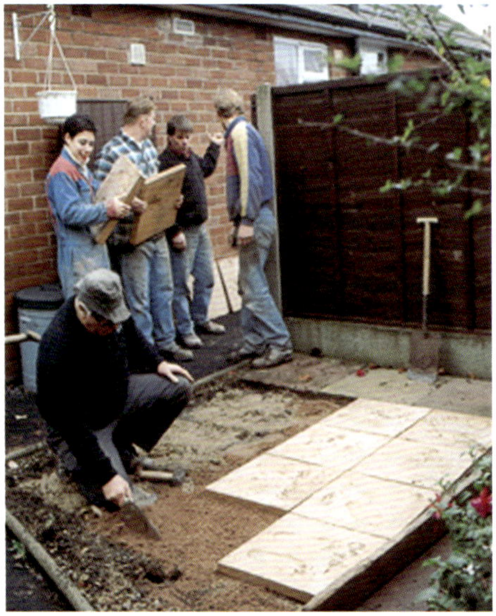

Gary Cook fitted the bill perfectly. A 'pool fanatic from the age of four, Gary's car number plate, GAZ 2 5 53, reminds him daily of the date when Blackpool FC won the FA Cup. When Jessica first met Gary on the windswept sands of Blackpool pleasure beach. She showed him some examples of her previous work, including photographs of herself posing with a waxwork model of DJ Chris Evans. "Do you see this as art?", Jessica asked. "To be honest, no", answered Gary, somewhat nervously.

Jessica wanted to make something that would (literally) create a very concrete and personal link between Gary and the team who he – along with hundreds of other anonymous fans on the terraces – would normally worship from afar. "One aspect of being a fan", recognised Jessica, "is wanting to own anything that has to do with the person you idolise, anything they've touched becomes worthy of keeping."

Putting these two ideas together, Jessica decided to make a work based on Graumann's Chinese Theatre on Sunset Boulevard in Hollywood, where famous movie stars consider it a mark of status to be invited to leave their imprint on the sidewalk. In Jessica's transatlantic version, the players of Blackpool FC were cast in the role of Cary Grant and Humphrey Bogart and Sunset Boulevard became Gary's back yard. Although it meant stripping off on a raw November day and sticking their feet (or, in the goalie's case, hands) into lumps of freezing concrete, the players were only too happy to do their bit in the name of art. "They were all very charming and co-operative", said Jessica: a revelation that will, no doubt, surprise the odd referee.

Despite its unconventional form, Jessica hoped that the outcome would be a piece of contemporary art that Gary could relate to. "People sometimes get aggressive about art because they feel that it's some kind of insider language which excludes them from understanding. This piece of work, when it goes into Gary's garden, will be exactly what it appears to be: a souvenir of his football club, and a piece of garden furniture. It will be a very personal piece to him. The meaning is right there on the surface and very easy to tap into."

The work was unveiled to Gary when he arrived home from a 2-1 victory over local rivals Burnley. Would it be a winning night all round? "Oh yes, Oh brilliant, Oh bloody hell, I love it. That is definitely a work of art." was Gary's emphatic response. "We'll have to find somewhere else to put our new table now, we can't cover that up."

Jessica's relief was palpable: "I was really worried", she confessed, "because you said if I gave you a pile of bricks you'd think 'what a load of bollocks'." Clearly, the forward-thinking football-fan of today prefers his contemporary art in concrete.

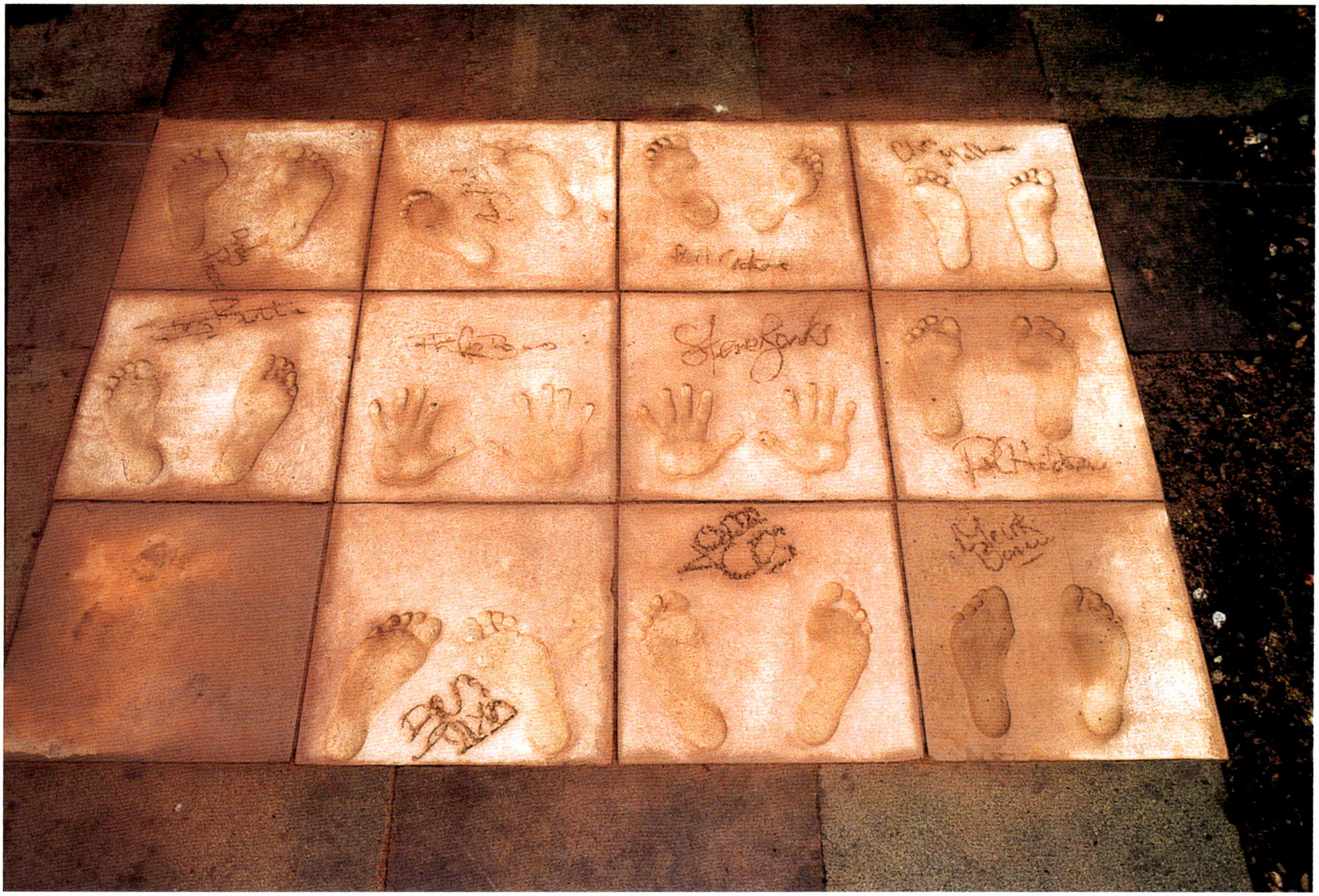

WHERE TO SEE AND READ ABOUT CONTEMPORARY AND MODERN ART...

PLACES TO SEE CONTEMPORARY ART IN THE OPEN AIR

Ambleside: Grizedale Sculpture in the Forest, Hawkshead - t: 01229 860291
Forest of Dean: Sculpture Trail - t: 01594 833057
Goodwood: Sculpture at Goodwood, Hat Hill - t: 01243 538449
Wakefield: Yorkshire Sculpture Park, Bretton Hall - t: 01924 830302

MAGAZINES ON CONTEMPORARY ART AND PHOTOGRAPHY

Art Monthly: t: 0171 240 0389
Art Review: t: 0171 236 4880
Artists Newsletter: t: 0191 567 3589
Creative Camera: t: 0171 729 6993
Dazed & Confused: t: 0171 336 0766
Frieze: t: 0171 379 1533
Make (the magazine of womens' art): t: 0171 731 7618
Modern Painters: t: 0171 636 6058
Portfolio: t: 0131 220 1911
Tate: t: 0171 706 4596
Mute: t: 0171 613 4743

BOOKS ON MODERN & CONTEMPORARY ART

Art & The Home, Art & Design, Academy Group Ltd, London, 1996
Art in Theory 1900-1990 - ed. Harrison & Wood, Blackwell Publishers, Oxford, 1992
British Art Since 1900 - Frances Spalding, Thames and Hudson, London, 1986
Installation Art - ed. Nicolas de Oliveira - Thames and Hudson, London, 1994
Moving Targets: A User's Guide to British Art Now - Louisa Buck, Tate Gallery Publishing, London, 1997
Rachel Whiteread: House - ed. James Lingwoood, Phaidon Press, London, 1995
Shark Infested Waters - Sarah Kent, Zwemmer, London, 1994
The Story of Modern Art - Norbert Lynton, Phaidon Press, London, 1980
Women, Art and Society - Whitney Chadwick, Thames and Hudson, London, 1990

CONTEMPORARY ART GALLERIES

LONDON:

Camden Arts Centre, Arkwright Road, NW3 - t: 0171 435 5224
Chisenhale Gallery, 64 Chisenhale Road, E3 - t: 0181 981 4518
Hayward Gallery, South Bank, SE1 - t: 0171 960 4208
Institute of Contemporary Arts (ICA), The Mall, SW1 - t: 0171 930 3647
Photographers' Gallery, Great Newport Street, WC2 - t: 0171 831 1772
Saatchi Gallery, Boundary Road, NW8 - t: 0171 624 8299
Serpentine Gallery, Kensington Gardens, W2 - t: 0171 402 6075
South London Gallery, Peckham Road, SE5 - t: 0171 703 6120
Tate Gallery, Millbank, SW1P - t: 0171 887 8000
Whitechapel Art Gallery, Whitechapel High Street, E1 - t: 0171 522 7878
(see Time Out listings for up-to-date exhibitions information and information more local venues)

ELSEWHERE IN THE UK:

Belfast: Ormeau Baths Gallery, Ormeau Avenue - t: 01232 321402
Birmingham: Ikon Gallery, Oozells Square - t: 0121 643 0708
Brighton: Brighton Museum & Art Gallery, Church Street - t: 01273 290900
Bristol: Arnolfini, Narrow Quay - t: 0117 929 9191
Cambridge: Cambridge Darkroom Gallery, Gwydir Street - t: 01223 566725
Canterbury: The Herbert Read Gallery, New Dover Road - t: 01227 769371
Cardiff: Chapter Arts Centre, Market Road - t: 01222 396061
Cardiff: Ffotogallery, Charles Street - t: 01222 341667
Colchester: Firstsite at the Minories, High Street - t: 01206 577067
Derry: Orchard Gallery, Orchard Street - t: 01504 269675
Eastbourne: Towner Art Gallery, High Street - t: 01323 417961
Edinburgh: Fruitmarket Gallery, Market Street - t: 0131 225 2383
Edinburgh: Portfolio Gallery, Candlemaker Row - t: 0131 220 1911
Exeter: Spacex Gallery, Preston Street - t: 01392 431786
Glasgow: Centre for Contemporary Art, Sauchiehall Street - t: 0141 332 7521
Glasgow: Tramway, Albert Drive - t: 0141 422 2023
Halifax: Dean Clough Galleries - t: 01422 250250
Leeds: Henry Moore Institute, The Headrow - t: 0113 247 8248
Liverpool: Bluecoat Gallery, School Lane - t: 0151 709 5689
Liverpool: Tate Gallery Liverpool, Albert Dock - t: 0151 709 3223
Llandudno: Oriel Mostyn Gallery, Vaughan Street - t: 01492 879201
Lymington: ArtSway, Station Road, Sway - t: 01590 682260
Manchester: Cornerhouse, Oxford Street - t: 0161 228 7162
Newcastle-Upon-Tyne: Zone Gallery, Westgate Road - t: 0191 232 8833
Norwich: Norwich Gallery, St. George Street - t: 01603 610561
Nottingham: Angel Row Gallery, Angel Row - t: 0115 947 6334
Oxford: Museum of Modern Art, Pembroke Street - t: 01865 722733
Sheffield: Site Gallery, Brown Street - t: 0114 272 5947
Southampton: John Hansard Gallery, University of Southampton - t: 01703 59
St. Ives: Tate Gallery St. Ives, Porthmeor Beach - t: 01736 796226
Sunderland: Northern Gallery for Contemporary Art, Fawcett St. - t: 0191 514 1235
Walsall: Walsall Museum & Art Gallery, Lichfield Street - t: 01922 653116
York: Impressions Gallery, Castlegate - t: 01904 651509